PUNCH GUIDE TO GOOD LIV

Also edited by William Davis, and available in Coronet Books:

THE PUNCH BEDSIDE BOOK

Copyright © by Punch Publications Limited
First published by Punch Publications Limited
Coronet edition 1973

Printed and bound in Great Britain for
Coronet Books,
Hodder Paperbacks Ltd,
St. Paul's House, Warwick Lane,
London, EC4P 4AH
by Hazell Watson & Viney Ltd,
Aylesbury, Bucks

ISBN 0 340 18215 6

The Punch Guide to Good Living

Edited by
William Davis

CORONET BOOKS
Hodder Paperbacks Ltd., London

CONTENTS

4

Introduction

There was a young lady of Kent
Who said she knew what it meant
When men asked her to dine
Gave her cocktails and wine,
She knew what it meant—but she went!

THERE should be no doubt about the meaning of this book either. Like our Bedside Book last year (which dealt mainly with the pleasures of Bed) it is intended to lead you astray. It will appal ascetics whose world is devoted to yoghourt and lettuce, and who regard Good Living as evil. But it may give you some useful ideas, and help you to follow Jonathan Swift's advice to "live all the days of your life".

The articles and cartoons have appeared in Punch over many years, and I have resisted the urge to tamper with them. So if you find cartoons which strike you as out of date, and references to long-forgotten events, don't worry. Good Living is not a new invention, and I hope you will find it both entertaining and instructive to make comparisons with the life-style of earlier generations.

Going through the many volumes in the Punch Library, as I did in the course of preparing this book, is a pleasant experience. They are a unique social record, a fascinating commentary on the habits and attitudes of British men and women over a period of more than 130 years. This is particularly true of the cartoons, but the articles and verses are just as interesting. I thoroughly enjoyed, for example, Thackeray's three essays on the pleasures of the Dinner Table and I have included them in the firm belief that you will find them equally charming. There's also a short article, by an unnamed author, "on the eating of asparagus", which I found in an old volume entitled "Mr. Punch in Mayfair".

But Punch is not simply a monument to the past. No weekly magazine could possibly survive unless it concerned itself very much with the present. We do so—in our own way. And we have a lot of fun in the process. The Punch editorial office is unlike any of the newspaper offices I have ever worked in. It would be absurd for a humorous magazine to stand on ceremony, to have an air of brisk efficiency and solemn concern for the cares of the world. There has to be a little room for lunacy. We get up to some crazy things, but we have a marvellous time. It's our idea of Good Living.

The first four editors of Punch were men of ample girth, and today the tradition is continued by regular contributors like Robert Morley, Harry Secombe and William Hardcastle. Naturally, you will find articles by all three in this book.

There was a time when Englishmen were renowned for their appetite: we were men of substance. Today, newspapers and magazines are obsessed by calories. Day after day, week after week, they do their best to make us feel bad about eating. Like so much else, this habit has been picked up from the Americans. The sole purpose, as far as I can see, is to ensure that we fit into ludicrously tight and absurdly uncomfortable pants. For this we struggle, for this we become as bad-tempered and neurotic as our alleged cousins across the Atlantic. It is gratifying, therefore, to give space to the few writers who have courage enough to protest.

Mind you, true gluttony is not merely a matter of eating sixty pickled onions in fifteen minutes thirty seconds, or having ten drinks when everyone else is content to make do with one. The really accomplished glutton does not eat just to dispose of food, or drink simply to establish some kind of record, or even to take maximum advantage of the fact that party booze happens to be free. He strives to combine quality with quantity—and he doesn't care whether his performance is watched by an audience.

In Paris, some time ago, I sat next to a master of the art of gluttony. He was totally oblivious of his surroundings; his concentration on the business in hand was complete. The rest of the world had ceased to exist. Two waiters kept bringing one course after another, and he never deigned to acknowledge them. Napkin tucked firmly under his chin, table well away from the already formidable stomach, he went through eighteen oysters, a large silver salver full of prawns, an equally large bowl of *moules marinière,* a whole lobster, a vast salad, a Camembert large enough for four, a bottle and a half of Rosé, a double brandy, coffee and two considerable cigars without saying a word, or giving anyone else a glance. He respected his food: he did not read, or spoil his enjoyment by chatting to friends or waiters. And he gave himself plenty of time. The only outward sign of the turmoil which must have been going on within was the colour of his face, which changed from an indifferent shade of white to pink, then red, then purple as the meal progressed.

When he finally got up from the table, the waiters jumped forward—pumped his hand, congratulated him on what was obviously a daily show, and ushered him out with a deference seldom accorded to an ordinary customer. He was an expert, a trencherman of the first rank, and the admiring glances of the waiters, and the crowd, seemed no more than his due.

In a nearby bar, that same evening, I saw another expert slowly and magnificently drinking himself into a stupor. His chosen medium was champagne, and he drank it from a large glass—not one of those thimbles so widely, and so wrongly, favoured by amateurs. He was alone, and he didn't bat an eyelid as he worked his way through the first bottle. A barely perceptible nod, and the barman promptly uncorked another.

He got through that, too, without breaking into song, telling a dirty joke, or smashing up the furniture. As he staggered out into the rain-soaked streets, I felt like cheering. And I did.

There's a Russian joke based on the well-known longevity of people in the Caucasus. Hearing about a 125-year-old man in one village, a journalist went to interview him. He asked him how he managed to live so long. Said the old man: "I never smoke. I never drink. I eat very little. And I have nothing to do with women". At that moment there was a frightful noise of crashing furniture, female giggling, exuberant male shouting, stamping, chasing. "What's that?" asked the startled journalist. "Oh," said the old man. "That's my older brother. He's drunk all the time."

Have fun.

WILLIAM DAVIS

"It's pollution but of a rather high order."

The Flesh-Pot Stakes

ALAN COREN

NOW that the days are drawing in, many of you will be sitting around a roaring hearth, swopping chestnuts and roasting tales and engaging in such heady philosophical discussions as Is Monarchy Dead? and Oliver Goldsmith: Last Of The Augustans Or First Of The Romantics? I know this, because I was an intellectual myself, once, and I still have the book somewhere; in those days (we were all gauche tyros and believed passionately that the world could be organised by theoreticians), a favourite topic for debate—we had all studied Greek—was What Do We Mean By The Good Life? Some of us were Platonists, some of us Ionians, some Aristotelians; some followed Aquinas, others Descartes, a few toyed with Leibniz, and more than one had locked into the transcendental criticism of Kant or the broody misgivings of Arthur Schopenhauer. But, as the sophistries flew back and forth above the Wincarnis, it always and inevitably emerged that our concept of The Good Life was the same. It was a blonde with a big bust who got giggly on one shandy.

Of course, all that was a decade ago, and time has mellowed me out of the follies of youth and its arrogant dogmatism. These days, she doesn't have to be blonde.

Philosophy, however, has as its concern the nature of states which are not, and the secondary occupation of relating these to states which are. I would therefore like to take the ideal of The Good Life, and illustrate its essence by a pragmatic example. Ten years ago, when I was at Yale, it was the practice of young English graduates eager to cross America and experience at first-hand the living myth of the illimitable West (that it was packed to the seams with teenage divorcees who outnumbered the male population by eighty to one), it was the practice, I say, of such pioneers to put ads in East Coast papers offering to ferry motor-cars to California for New Yorkers who preferred to fly rather than end up on some Minnesotan freeway as humanberry jam. My own ad, craftily worded to give the impression of the worder as a circumspect total abstainer who had thrice crossed the world at thirty-five mph, brought a flood of replies, giving me the opportunity to choose a '61 Oldsmobile 88 convertible, which I personally knew to be capable of being gunned up to 130 with a kind hand on the tiller. It was primrose yellow, and had just been picked up from the showroom by two elderly residents of Groton, Conn., who were retiring to Santa Monica.

I had hardly separated them from their phaeton than I was out of my pinstripe disguise and into my real travelling gear;

and I don't mind saying that as I swung west on the Jersey pike, I cut a fairly memorable dash. I was better-looking in those days, and a lot taller, and blessed with a crop of thick curly hair that had made my shine the talk of Kampus Klothes Inc. when I stopped by for the polka-dotted Bermudas that now glazed my thighs. I won't bore you with sartorial details of my upper frame, not when there's so much else to bore you with, but suffice it to say that with the 88 ripping along at a hundred and the radio knocking the magpies off the phone-wires and a king-size Lucky gummed to my upper lip, and my bare arm hanging nonchalantly over the side (where it was soon turned to a healthy tan by several layers of smashed flies), I was the very picture of a Good Life stud, lacking only the complement of something svelte and windswept in the seat beside me.

I finally picked her up at a gas-station outside Akron, Ohio. She was big, blonde, and seventy-three. The pump-jockey had come out and winked and said There's a dame inside needs a ride, and I had winked and said Suits me, and then she sprang out from behind a Coke dispenser with four suitcases and hopped in. She hopped out again six hundred miles further on, in Cedar Rapids, Iowa, but not before she had converted me to Jansenism and taught me thirty-nine words of colloquial Pawnee.

It was a lesson I was to be given, if not taught, many times during the subsequent decade: that The Good Life Lies Within Each And Every One Of Us. And that's where it ought to stay; getting it out is where the problems start. (At this juncture, if that's where we are, it ought to be said that I do not intend touching upon that concept of The Good Life which involves walking about in a sack and helping one's fellow-man: diverting as that may be, it has nothing to do with the real Good Life, which is self-sacrificing, tough, ruinous to health, and shot through with a brand of total dedication that would have left St. Francis two furlongs down the field, and fading. About the only monk ever to have come close was Rasputin).

The first and greatest problem to recognise, if not overcome, is that The Good Life should really be known as The Best Life, since it is an ideal, a summit, not a stage or a comparative. It is a superlative to aim at, and one of the snags is that they keep dragging the target further away, just when you think you've drawn a bead on it. This is because The Good Life is entirely to do with money, even when it's to do with sex, liquor, food or anything else: that is to say, if you are belting down to Cannes in a Porsche 911 with a dolly who has graced the gatefold of *Penthouse*, it may be said that you are leading The Good Life. But only until that moment when you are passed by a bloke in a Ferrari Dino who is belting down to Cap Ferat with a dolly who has graced the gatefold of *Playboy*. Because he has redefined The Good Life (i.e. The

Best Life) for you. And as far as he's concerned, he's doing fine until he has to pull over for a Lamborghini Miura belting down to Antibes with a dolly who has turned down both *Penthouse* and *Playboy*, despite the fact that they keep ringing up in the small hours and raising the ante. There is nothing worse than being involved in a slice of Good Life that hasn't *quite* made it. Time, I feel, for a further shot of pragmatism.

Before I was married (I hope), I happened to fall in with a fairly racy crowd, one of whom invited me down to Monte Carlo to watch the Monaco Grand Prix and while away the evenings on his yacht with as much of the local nubilia as we could winch aboard. It was a good yacht as yachts go, which is to say it didn't, and that suited me very well, since I am a great sailor at anchor: we merely lolled in the azure harbour, boozing and braising, while the cars nattered angrily through the nearby town, like trapped wasps. As the sun began to dip beneath the yard-arm, I think they said it was, we four good livers hailed a couple of the circling pedalos with which the environment was dotted, and were joined by four attractive locals; of, I think, Wembley. All was proceeding splendidly, despite the fact that these lovelies turned out to have hollow legs and were taking in Bollinger with all the chic gusto of a bilge-pump, and the evening's auguries were good.

It was at about eight p.m. that I grew suddenly aware that the setting sun had been blotted out. I glanced up, to find that a thing had moored alongside us that would have given the *Bismarck* a run for its money; I had my hand on a knee at the time, and I felt it lurch within my palm. At that moment, a

"If this is declining then it sure beats progress."

11

Ninth Officer or some such leaned over the bridge of this leviathan, took aim with a loudhailer which must have broken windows as far away as Genoa, and asked us to join them for drinks. The knee was out of my palm and sprinting before the last echo had died away towards Algeria, closely followed by seven others. Since the dory would not hold eight, the four girls were gallantly rowed across first, and my friend returned for the three other men.

We never saw the birds again. By the time we had climbed aboard our host, there was nothing on the afterdeck but about forty middle-aged men in Pucci shirts, their faces the colour and consistency of old wallets and enough gold in their assembled bicuspids to take over General Motors. Since it was clear that, as soon as our last plimsoll had touched the deck, we had outstayed our welcome, we were back aboard our own tub, as it had proved to be, in less time than it takes to tell, where we spent the remainder of the night playing Scrabble by the light of the ostentatious navigation beacon next door, some way beneath which our erstwhile dollies were being shown, as it were, the ropes. Sorry, they're called sheets in sailing circles, aren't they?

The thing is, The Good Life is not for amateurs. It is either for dreamers or for professional participants, and it is a mistake to jump that enormous chasm that separates the two unless you're good and sure of landing on both feet on the other side, with cash in hand and plenty more where that came from.

And, should you be naive enough to require consolation, always remember that even those who most appear to be actively engaged in leading The Good Life, aren't in fact doing so. They're still only looking for it, really.

"This is the life, eh?"

It is Better to Travel First Class than to arrive...

LORD MANCROFT votes for luxury

WHETHER you can afford it or not, you should always travel first class to which you will naturally transfer.

I was confirmed recently in this view by my old friend Charlie Cringleford. Now the Noble Lord, Lord Cringleford, though an excellent judge of port, is unfortunately an indifferent judge of racehorses and these two qualifications have prevented him from amassing much of a fortune. Although I was naturally delighted to find that he was a fellow passenger on a recent flight to New York, I was slightly surprised to see him heading like myself for the snobbier end of the plane. I, of course, was travelling at the shareholders' expense but Charlie, I knew, would be paying his own whack. I'm afraid, however, that I failed to disguise my surprise.

"Yes, indeed," he said when we were settled down to our Bloody Marys. "I used to travel steerage but I shall never do it again. I've learned my lesson. Last time I did it I had to spend seven hours in the heart of a Pakistani family reunion. Nomadic types too, they were. Fidgety. Up and down the whole time. And as for the food. Oh Lord! Nourishing enough but I've never really cared for Gutta percha sandwiches and purée of boot polish."

And though of course I realise that they've got to pack 'em in those kitchen chairs they give you in steerage class—"Charlie" I said, "it's economy class not steerage and the seats are carefully designed to comply with international requirements. Nor is it really the fault of IATA that you yourself are constructed so nearly on the architectural principles of the Albert Hall that they have to take the plane apart and reconstruct it every time you want to wash your hands."

"All right," said Charlie, "I will ignore that insult although it reveals yet another reason for travelling first. I don't wish to appear unfriendly but I definitely do not relish standing for twenty minutes in the loo queue, squadged into the midst of a bevy of Pakistani beauties." Charlie paused. "I say, be a good fellow and ask the stewardess to put a smidgeon more celery salt in my next Bloody Mary and tell her, will you, that I'm going to have the Chambolle Musigny with my *sole Dieppoise*

13

*". . . Sir, it's amazing . . . the moment you walked through
that door I said, Victor Blackthorpe, I said, you've found the
one man in this city who could give your chair the quiet
dignity it so desperately needs to justify the exquisite
craftsmanship that created this hand-stitched masterpiece on
easy terms . . . !"*

and the Aloxe Corton with the pheasant. Now, what about
you?"

Charlie of course is right. Long distance air travel is
remarkable value for money but the journey is never a joyride
and if you have any regard for your comfort and, that most
unattainable of all luxuries, privacy, the difference in price
between first and economy class, though wide, is worth it.

The Russians, incidentally, have a different approach to the
problem of the loo queue. I was flying once between
Leningrad and Kiev and although the weather was perfect the
pilot frequently switched on what I had by then learned to
recognise as the "fasten your seat belt" sign. I eventually
discovered the reason for this. To save weight and space,
Russian designers have kept their aircraft pretty low on loos so
the loo load factor is consequentially high. When therefore the
crew themselves want to wash their hands they slip on the seat
belt sign to ensure the competition is safely battened down.

The service and food in Russian aircraft is indescribable but
this is because all Russian service and food is indescribable

and not because the Russians have to comply with IATA regulations.

The service and food, however, in the Monarch class of BOAC is of a very high order indeed and a luncheon there can turn a routine journey into genuine pleasure. Panam, Air India and KLM all run BOAC pretty close, but there's nothing new in standards such as these. The Paris service of Imperial Airways in the twenties was luxurious even by modern standards. The scoff was laid on to match and there wasn't, thank heavens, any Musak.

Today the VC 10 is the most comfortable aircraft flying, but even that machine would be hard put to beat the old Short Sunderland flying boat. This aeroplane had a separate dining room, a comfortable dormitory upstairs and it brought you gently down on some romantic waterway each night of the eight-day journey to Australia. They also produced a marvellous curry tiffin but you were lucky not to get it in your lap if you got caught in a monsoon over the Arakan. The old bucket could bounce like blazes—even up in the first class.

At sea, the class distinction used to be formidable. "Port out, Starboard home" gave memsahib the shady side of the ship and the word Posh to the English language. Cunard's pursers were instructed to have the steerage emigrants scrubbed on the quayside at Liverpool in order to ensure that they arrived bugless in Boston. But the fare was only £4.10.

The first-class passengers, however, had to wear white ties for dinner but they had 26 brands of champagne to choose from. Their linen sheets were changed each night though not, we hope, scrubbed.

Most new passenger liners today are classless. A few, like QE2, are dual purpose ships; two classes across the Atlantic and classless whilst cruising. This interchangeability makes it difficult to persuade people to travel first because the class distinction appears to be so slight. But I can assure you it's worth it because in the real first class you get limitless caviare and a nice little fridge in your stateroom.

The QE2's problem arises again in our trains. British Railways' new rolling stock is nearly as comfortable in second class as it is in first but although both classes invariably go on strike at the same time, there's still a valid reason for travelling first and that, of course, is breakfast.

BR's breakfast is a wonderful meal and if they could only serve breakfast at lunch and dinner, British Rail would have the best mobile cuisine in the world. Not that their other meals are all that bad. They do occasionally serve up the piece of cod that passeth all understanding but a lot may be forgiven a chef who has to juggle with boiling fat at 80 m.p.h.

Always travel first class rail between Washington and New York; it's much more comfortable than the air and oddly enough it's faster. Be a devil too and travel de luxe by CPR from Vancouver. Their scenic car gives you a view of the

Rockies that's even more spectacular than the brochure proclaims and it's nice having a moose watching you shave.

It's difficult to define class in hotels. Too many hotels are now just body-serving units and luxury consists in being able to leave a hotel without standing in line for twenty minutes for the privilege of paying your bill. I'm all for electric razor sockets, of course, as well as ice-making machines in the passage and tooth glasses specially sterilised for my personal protection, but sometimes I miss the old-fashioned night-porter and his comments on the 3.30 at Kempton Park.

In most modern hotels real luxury can only mean real service. I own a rather disreputable pair of leather slippers which are useful for kicking-off in aeroplanes. Despite my wife's protests that we should lose face, I put them outside our door to be cleaned when we were last staying in the superb Mandarin Hotel in Hong Kong. They were duly returned in the morning, not only shining like the *Morning Star* but soled and heeled as well. That I call très grande luxe.

But luxury in travel is relative. Was the outside of the Edinburgh stage coach in a howling blizzard over the Yorkshire moors considered grander than the sardine-packed and pongful interior? And in any case, both classes ran an equal risk of being held up by Dick Turpin proclaiming, "Your money or your life" which is the olde Englishe for "Excuse please, if you do not fly this aircraft to Cuba immediately, I will be forced to blow out your brains."

I must apologise to all potential steerage passengers for the bloatedly plutocratic advice that I have been offering. I should, however, also like to offer one final word by way of recompense.

BOAC own a miraculous piece of telecommunication juju named Boadicea which, at the punch of a key, can tell you the load factor of next Wednesday's flight out of Boston or the names of those who are travelling first-class this afternoon to Johannesburg. One day I was watching Boadicea at work and up on the screen popped the name of my old friend Jimmy X, apparently South Africa-bound. I remarked to BOAC's men, "I did not realise that my friend X had interests in the Cape." "No," said BOAC. "You have misread the data. Observe the asterisk against your friend's name. That indicates he is disembarking in Rome.

Two days later I ran across Lady X at a party. "And how is that old rascal Jimmy enjoying himself in Rome?" enquired Mr. Know All. "Rome?" replied a slightly puzzled Lady X. "Jimmy's not in Rome. He's fishing up in Scotland."

You do not run that sort of risk in steerage.

"I have scoured the Midlands looking for a belly-dancer, and I can't find one anywhere," Mr. Watts said. *(Birmingham Mail)*

Tense up and live!

GILLIAN TINDALL

THE myth has got around that r-e-l-a-x-a-t-i-o-n always spells something good.

"The drink/chocolates/interior springs with which you can really relax" cry the adverts. "The place for a really relaxing holiday" insist brochures with pictures of people doing nothing expensively in colour; while pregnant women facing what may be a formidable ordeal somehow imbibe the false impression that to have a baby successfully all you really have to do is—relax.

Yet if you look up relax in the Oxford dictionary what it says is "cause or allow to become loose or slack or limp, enfeeble, enervate, mitigate, abate"—none of which sounds particularly desirable or satisfying, does it? Do quite so many people need to relax as seem to think they do? Helping people to do it has become an industry in which not only the luxury trades but the National Health Service itself is involved to the tune of many million pounds a year. If you go to a doctor complaining that you feel unaccountably tired, depressed, irritated or dissatisfied, what you are almost certain to come away with is something "to help you to relax". Yet it is common knowledge in the medical profession that many "depressed" patients are suffering not from too much going on in their lives but too little: their real need is not to be made less tense but to be given something worth being tense about—for which, unfortunately, there is no simple prescription.

The ultimate index to this problem is the suicide figures. In any prosperous, relatively peaceful society like ours suicide rates tend to be fairly high, far higher than in backward societies where people have urgent things to worry about like where the next meal is coming from. (No moral to be drawn from this, I suggest.) Yet in time of war or similar crisis Western suicide rates go right down. In war, people tend to suffer from all sorts of privations, griefs and separations, frustrations and overwork—and yet, it seems, there is nothing like a good solid war for curing much of the nebulous depression in society.

We have become so accustomed to hearing the word "tension" used pejoratively, as the opposite of "relaxation," that we tend to lose sight of the fact that, strictly speaking, a degree of tension is necessary and that nobody accomplishes anything without it. You have to be tense—sufficiently tense—to be motivated to write a book, paint a picture, learn a language, even to cook a meal. A totally "relaxed" person would be a disaster, since he would lack any motivation to do anything but exist minimally. Well—totally relaxed people *are* a disaster, aren't they, for their families and ultimately for themselves?

The funny thing is that, secretly, we all know this. Most people are quite well aware of the need to pull themselves up by their own bootstraps to achieve their goal, whether that goal is six nice children, six operas, six girls at once, six boutiques in the King's Road, or just more money. Secretly, a lot of us spend quite a bit of our time vigilantly working and/ or intriguing to gain these or similar ends. Yet because crude words like "hard work," "ambition"—and "goal" itself—are out of fashion, we dissemble. We pretend to be above such earnest striving (another unfashionable phrase). We may, if we are particularly self-conscious about our image, publicly extol letting go, keeping cool, getting away from it all, dropping out, leaving the rat-race, losing our hang-ups—whatever expression is most acceptable in our particular circle. Secretly, if we're honest, we know it's a con. Hang-ups are what makes life interesting. Nor is it only worthy attainments that have to be worked for. The Beatles didn't get there by keeping cool—don't let them kid you.

If you analyse the "relaxing holiday" people say they want, you usually find that what they really have in mind is an activity like ski-ing (snow or water), dancing every night, having an adventure or "getting to know the people," all of which require sustained energy and skill. There is nothing like a holiday *really* doing nothing to make all concerned thoroughly bad-tempered with each other before the first week is out. Comparatively few people actually need to "rest," enormous numbers need to do something quite *different* from what they usually do, but equally, if not more, strenuous. More seriously, if you retire to a quiet place at sixty-five with the intention of doing nothing gently for the rest of your days, you court premature senility. Abilities need to be used, at any age, or they go bad on you.

I offer no apologies for these old-fashioned remarks, since I have a strong suspicion that my particular version of old-fashionedness will come to be much more widely acknowledged again than it is at present, long before I'm sixty myself.

In our new frank society the widespread, hidden vice of enjoying hard work surely cannot hope to remain a shameful secret indefinitely?

"Home of the Happy People"

For a honeymoon, a tenth anniversary, or a twenty-fifth, it [Tahiti] is clearly the spot *sans pareil*.
Join in a *Tamaaraa*, the Tahitian feast. Thrill to a Tahitian dance. Ride an outrigger canoe. Climb Mr. Tohivea."—*An airlines brochure.*

The *happy* Mr. Tohivea?

Cakes and Ale

**R. G. G. Price examines
the Punch approach to high living**

WHAT our forefathers meant by the Good Life varied
with whether they were talking Religion in public or
praising wine, women and song in private. The saintly, of
course, set themselves a high standard of discomfort; but this
was apt to lead to imposing discomfort on others. Not everybody in Victorian England was prepared to take his code of
conduct from birch-happy clerical headmasters. For the
dissentients, there was a rival tradition which combined kindness to neighbours with cheerful self-indulgence the tradition
of Dickens.

Punch in its early days followed in Dicken's footsteps. The
Good Life included both benevolence and liquor, attacks on
court flunkies and musical sessions in bars, denunciations of
cruel workhouse masters and gluttony at Christmas. The paper
was prepared to pay lip service to some of the more taxing

Juvenis. *"Jolly day we had last week at McFoggarty's
Wedding! Capital Champagne he gave us, and we
did it justice, I can tell you—"*
Senex (who prefers Whisky). *"Eh—h, Mun, it's a' vera weel
weddings at ye—er time o' life. Gie me a solid
Funeral!"*

1867

Of the World Worldly

(*Scene*—The Entrance Hall of Sir Gorgius Midas's London residence.)

Mamma. *"Enfin, my love! We're well out of this!! What a gang!!! Where shall we go next?"*

Daughter. *"To Lady Oscar Talbot's, Mamma?"*

Mamma. *"She snubs one so! I really can't bear it! Let us go to Mrs. Ponsonby de Tomkyns'. It's just as select (except for the Host and Hostess), and quite as amusing."*

Daughter. *"But Mrs. Tomkyns snubs one worse than Lady Oscar, Mamma!"*

Mamma. *"Pooh, my love! Who cares for the snubs of a* Mrs. Ponsonby de Tomkyns, *I should like to know, so long as she's clever enough to get the right people!"*

1879

Christian ideals; but it distrusted enthusiasm, as it distrusted ritualism. It believed less in the egocentric austerities of the hermit than in the warm kindness and warm indignation of an average, decent man in a world containing, at one extreme, aristocrats served on gold plate by powdered footmen and, at the other, slum children, death by starvation, military flogging and bad drains.

Despite the recent spate of information about the sex life of the Victorians, their tastes in cakes and ale were not exclusively erotic. A far from exhaustive list of pleasures can be compiled from Punch:—a cigar with the brandy after a good meal, catching the fish which the innkeeper's wife will dress for dinner, invitations to the better houses, the quaint remarks of children, parsons and the Irish, showing off one's furniture, vigorous dances, family picnics on the beach, cubbing in the morning mists, croquet with delicately nurtured and quite unscrupulous girls, the music hall, overeating and sensational law reports.

By the end of the century, the Good Life included Rowing, which provided healthy exercise, soothing scenery and a chance of showing off to a feminine audience. Women had become Meredithian goddesses rather than Dickensian dolls or grotesques. Banter in conservatories with splendid girls led to marriages which were not traps but partnerships. Shrews and naggers *apparently* died out, except for slum harridans, a limited and localised class. Now paterfamilias pottered about the house, instead of returning from his club only just in time to meet his children before they went to bed. Carving on Sunday, with energies stoked up by the sermon, was no longer the husband's sole domestic activity. Gardening, hammering nails into the home and politely feuding with the neighbours also enjoyably filled his time.

During those golden summers before World War I, Punch and the people it represented ceased to be so hotly involved in reform. Politics became a matter of standing on the sidelines and being rude about politicians. The paper was now a spectator, often a disapproving one, not a participant. Indeed it sometimes seemed to see itself as an escape from the grown-up world of DUTY. The ideal existence was frankly hedonistic, and more to the taste of advertisers than to that of saints.

"Remember our first meal together, when we sat on soap-boxes and ate off tea-chests?"

Gross Hospitality

" 'Ave a cigar?"

In the days of Du Maurier's *nouveaux riches*, Sir Gorgius Midas and the rest, the cost of one's possessions was something to boast about: in this century it became a cause for groans. The Good Life tended to include bearing alleged poverty with a gay courage. Changes in leisure activities as drawn in Punch reflect the shift from a rural to an urban culture: motoring replaced riding, golf and tennis replaced hunting and shooting, nightclubs and road-houses replaced inns. Butts were no longer persons unkind to the poor but persons unkind to the pleasure seeker.

During the twenties and thirties, A. P. Herbert kept alive, almost single-handed, the paper's tradition of bashing abuses,

and developed it by fighting for specific reforms. He attacked the licensing laws, the Entertainment Duty, prudish restrictions on bathing, officialese and, above all, the divorce laws, when he won in Parliament a campaign long waged in Punch. All these gaily fought wars were directed to improving the quality of life. More was needed than the removal of restrictions; but how much better it is to have limited reforms rather than hold everything up until the fundamental reconstruction of human society.

In the fifties, Punch, like the country generally, ceased to think of the Good Life as simply a matter of leisure. The two previous decades had been fiercely political, but only among a minority. It seemed to me at the time that acceptance of civic responsibilities as a part of living became more widespread, influencing, for instance, popular fiction. Of course, there was a superficial trendiness in many cases: over exotic wines, people with a fascinated interest in their life-patterns disapproved of Affluence—a soul-destroying state of wishfulfillment enjoyed mainly by other people. This was recognised and mocked and died out. The permanent gain was that the idea of the Good Life as something irresponsible, private and immature was no longer tenable.

We are now in the seventies, unless my watch has stopped and elsewhere in this issue some assistance is given in coming to terms with the Good Life here and now.

"It's been a good life."

Alan Brien

Invents the perfect drink

EVERY time I am faced with a bar, I think: the second thing this country needs is a good, simple, new drink for half-a-crown. I take it all of you out there agree with me that you cannot do much better than a straightforward Scotch whisky. But even this is easier said than ordered. All you would appear to require is a bottle of the stuff, a glass and a cold tap. A piece of ice? Well, *en principe oui*, which is a French phrase meaning "no". If the weather is boiling, or if you are trying to slow down your intake, or if your host is showing off his refrigerator, then OK. But if you actually like the taste, as I do, it is enough to be presented with an old-fashioned glass of Scotch, topped up, in the proportion sixty/forty, with water as chilly as mains can manage. Almost nothing could be easier to arrange, but how rarely does such a drink ever actually arrive in your hand, whether served professionally or socially?

People who pass out drinks, like housewives who produce TV dinners or bake cakes from instant mixes, always want to demonstrate that they have personally added that final, secret, mystic, key ingredient which has transformed the concoction. So, having in front of them exactly what you need, they proceed to ruin it by throwing in raw eggs, HP sauce, tomato juice, slices of lemon, sprigs of mint and other garbage.

The American barman is, rightly, believed to be the world's expert in creating drinks. He stands there just itching to be asked to produce some such aromatic mishmash as a White Lady, a Pink Lady, a Sidecar, a Manhattan, a Gibson, a Green Goddess, a Moscow Mule, an Orange Blossom, a Tom Collins, a Clover Club or a Screwdriver—names that most British barmen would imagine to be runners in the 4.30, houseboats on the Norfolk Broads, or Olde Tyme dances. One reason for his eagerness to slave away over a misted shaker (some much-travelled drinking men say the only reason) is that he is usually given a tip after he has frothed it into your glass. "Mac," as he is always known, prides himself on never being fazed by a customer's request. Yet, to avoid being presented as a Scotch-and-water with a medium-sized flower vase, brim full of a dingy-beige rusty liquid, bulging with striated cubes, and tasting of yesterday's bedside carafe, I find I have to launch into a long, apologetic aria about my English origins. Even then, the barman removes the ice with his fingers, muttering under his breath.

Scotch is a noble invention, native to these isles and hard to fake under alien skies. It is at once oily and fiery, wholesome and dangerous, warming and numbing, like buttermilk gone mad. It is more dilutable than brandy (*usquebaugh* is the Gaelic for *eau-de-vie*) which smoulders across a warm palate like flaming treacle but is quickly quenched by a liberal addition of some mixer. Whisky retains its home-smoked flavour, like the Scots themselves, even when almost overpowered by invaders from across the Border. It will, it's true, succumb to ginger ale. But then who would miscegenate such a half-breed, except someone who really was looking for a nursery, sweet-toothed cordial with an underhand wallop? It was for him that vodka, the ghostly spirit, invisible, unsmellable, with that faint tang of thinned-down hydrochloric acid, was invented—the tipple of spies, the last refuge of closet topers.

But you, or at least I, cannot drink Scotch always and forever. It is Rolls-Royce fuel too potent for our Minis and Populars cruising the suburbs and trying for the highest mpg. Neat around 6 pm, it is an explosive pick-me-up—ideal for burning off the day's frustrations, especially on a touring holiday abroad, when no Continental liqueur can duplicate that energy-giving massage of the bruised psyche, battered by wrong turnings, false starts, mutinous children and an ominously understanding wife. Watered down at the end of a night on the town to an innocent imitation of cold tea, it becomes even more potent, mainlining itself into the blood stream quicker than a transfusion.

No, more often than not, in summer anyway, and on holiday, I am in search of some drink combining the most desirable properties of hard and soft liquor. I hanker after something long, faintly tart, yet fruity, thirst-quenching, sleep-defying, with a mild kick, which still does not cloy the palate. Every time I think I have found one, I realise that is exactly what I have found—one. I cannot stomach a second. They are perfect examples of that principle of academic economics, marginal utility, or do I mean the law of diminishing returns? Anyway, they satisfy too quickly.

I enjoy my first Screwdriver, savouring the rather fluffy, sunshine taste of the orange juice undermined by the keen medicinal bite of the vodka. A Bloody Mary is even more like food, thick and creamy, almost choking you like a swollen tongue, the quickest breakfast Kelloggs never made. Before lunch on a spring Sunday in New York, a Bullshot seems to leak into the gastric juices by osmosis, disdaining the long way round down the gullet, the alcohol preventing the beef consommé from being too meaty and gravy-rich. As mixed in the Bahamas, with fresh lime juice added, it is enough to wine and dine a man for the next six hours, becoming dessert as well as entrée. But I cannot imagine carrying on to ask for more. With these drinks, you always know when you have had enough.

Gin-based cocktails have their passionate partisans. But I find their basic ingredient thin, curdling and sour, the concentrated essence of old womanish malice. I have tried disguising it with the usual mixers, but bitter lemon is always too sweet, tonic water always too bland. Afterwards, I always feel mildly guilty, as if I had been pretending I was not really drinking, like a man sucking a peppermint lozenge on the way home from the pub.

Rum I must experiment with more seriously. When I used to sample it, during and just after the war, rum was always a rubicund sweetish brown, rather like toffee before it starts to thicken and harden. It was a child's idea of what an alcoholic spirit must be—the least sophisticated of drinks. White rum gives off a different aura, cool and subtle rather than hot and sticky, with an endearing affinity to citrus fruits. But here, too, I feel that all those sugar syrups and fruit cordials are over-egging the pudding when what I really want is something which can stand on its own, honest and unashamed.

Wine, I sometimes tell myself, must be the answer. But, firstly, this is not easy to find in pubs off the colour-supplement belt. When you do get it, the landlord seems obsessed by fear that the entire bottle will turn to vinegar half an hour after he has opened it, so he charges you danger money, SET, deterioration allowances, and a snob tax for having made him handle the volatile stuff. You get the impression that you are rather corrupting the tone of his bluff, English establishment by being seen with this sinister, foreign tipple. At 2s. 6d., sometimes 3s. 6d., a glass, he must be mak- a hefty profit on his eight-bob Château Sidi Bel Abbes, but you do not even get the credit of being a big spender.

I know nothing about fine wine, but I am an expert on superior plonk, having drunk a bottle a day of decent, ordinary, French grape juice for as long as I can remember. My palate is now so attuned to its coarse, strong, obvious appeal that I know when I am offered a really great wine because it tastes strange and unnatural. But whichever it is, wine revives rather than quenches thirst. I cannot help swigging it down in Bellocian draughts, and soon I am falling asleep as I swim, like a man adrift in the Atlantic. The same is true of beer, only more so. There is no reward more precious after a long walk than the first pint of some local brew, a little cloudy, just cooler than tepid, with the smell of the hop still floating on the surface, sucked up from a wooden barrel, not pursued along tinny pipes by bottled gas. But the second cancels out the first, and after the third you are there for the rest of the long evening.

I see now, as I write, that I am asking for a new drink with many contradictory, mutually exclusive, qualities. A drink that is long yet not filling, strong yet not incapacitating, fruity yet sugar-free, dilutable yet never drowned, habitual yet not addictive, cheap yet always reliable, stimulating yet soothing. Perhaps a mug of tea, piping hot or freshly iced, with a slurp of Scotch and a slice of lemon comes nearest to my formula. It is a big demand to make. But then so was a contraceptive pill. I still can hope that British ingenuity will not fail me.

The Morning After
by GRAHAM

"Aspirins . . ."

" 'Time to get up, Lazybones,'
she's saying."

"Give us a song then."

"This way! The station's this way!"

The Picnic Papers

HUMPHREY LYTTELTON al fresco

THE one really essential rule about a picnic is that you should ward off, with the ferocity of a tigress defending her young, the advice of any twit who thinks he can tell you how to make the most of a picnic. Having a picnic is one of those activities, like keeping a diary, which you must do in your own way or not at all. The *Concise Oxford Dictionary* is delightfully vague about the word "picnic" itself. It mumbles something about a "pleasure party including meal out of doors," gives the derivation as *pique-nique* (which is just saying the same thing in a Maurice Chevalier accent) and then hurries on to "picot," "picotee," "picquet" and "picric" with never a backward glance.

"Pleasure party including meal out of doors" seems to me to cover an almost limitless range of *al fresco* fun. But typically, the British make rather a fuss—a pique-nique mystique, if you like—about eating out of doors. The Catering Manager of BEA once told me that the whole of flight catering today is based on the observable fact that, regardless of when or how much he last ate, a passenger's first thought once the aircraft's wheels leave the runway is "Where's the food?"

It's much the same with the British and the open air—one whiff of bracken or glimpse of rabbit-droppings and it's out with the hamper and let's get stuck in. We have even managed, in our own inimitable way, to imbue the whole affair with several sorts of snobbery. We have *haute pique-nique* experts in the glossy mags to tell us how to make interesting sandwiches out of caviar and salmon left-overs and which Sauterne will go best with the peaches without attracting too many wasps. I suspect that few people pay attention to them. For our attitude to the picnic is Stoic rather than Epicurean.

The real picnic snob is the man who uses the event to show his contempt for civilisation in all its forms. He looks back to some mythical Golden Age when all men were boy scouts in flappy khaki shorts, fending for themselves without the aid of any of your namby-pamby modern inventions. ("That's you!" cried my family in unison when I read them this paragraph, but I don't see it. For one thing, my shorts are not flapping khaki but rather natty David Niven jobs—or were before somebody confiscated them). According to the picnic snob's code, Bracken and Twigs take precedence over Newspaper and Kindling Wood, Newspaper and Kindling Wood over Primus, Primus over Camping Gas, Camping Gas over Portable Barbecue and everything over Collapsible Table and Tea Cosy.

I have to tell him that history, insofar as we can interpret it from Art and Literature, is not on his side. I suppose Manet's

28

famous *Déjeuner sur l'Herbe* was a picnic within the meaning of the act, and whatever those glum-looking men in Sunday attire are up to with that naked lady in their midst, it certainly isn't roughing it.

In practically every classic English novel I ever read there is a point where one of the characters, presumably fed up with loafing about through two hundred and sixty pages without actually doing a thing, suggests a picnic and the lady of the house claps her hands and cries "Yes, a picnic it shall be!" Next morning, with a lot of female twittering and male flirting, a fleet of carriages sets off for some distant spot on the estate where the servants, presumably working all night, have erected tables, spread linen and set out a sumptuous repast. It must be noted that our heroes and heroines do not spend the morning scrabbling about for twigs, puffing like human bellows into a heap of lukewarm ashes, covering their finery with spitting fat and indulging in recriminations about who did or did not pack the salt. Their day, and the author's chapter, is spent eating a few refined mouthfuls, playing ball, wandering off into the shrubbery and generally, if rather tortuously, getting on with the plot.

If this is the genuine, prototype picnic—and it seems to fit the COD's definition pretty well—then we must accept that the leisurely repast in a layby off the A5, with the collapsible table erected in the lee of the Ford Anglia, fish paste in lieu of duck pâté and a tin-opener in lieu of servants, with Dad snoozing, Mum knitting, Gran watching the cars go by and the kids picking blackberries or trying to get Rover to do his business before the next leg of the journey, comes much closer to it than your boy scout safari. But as I said at the outset, a picnic is what you make of it, and if you want to make it an adventure-substitute, a military exercise involving the defusing of exploding sausages and the dodging of flying fat shrapnel, then good luck and don't fire till you see the whites of their eggs.

Me, I've done it all. When I was a schoolboy, my mother used to take me and a few chums on fry-ups in Windsor Great Park, cooking bacon in great lumps of lard and spicing the fried eggs with charred bracken. It all tasted lovely. The nearest I ever came to *haute pique-nique,* I suppose, was when as a young officer in the Grenadier Guards at Windsor I was sent, with five colleagues, to camp for three days by the Thames at Marlowe, presumably as some sort of toughening-up exercise. The Officers' Mess Sergeant at Victoria Barracks sent with us three huge packing cases full of food, drink, cutlery and crockery—and in the true picnic tradition, he forgot to pack anything to go with the gin. So we drank six bottles of port on the first night, researching the theory that *(a)* you get drunk quicker and *(b)* you have less of a hangover in the open air. Nobody thought to put a stopwatch on the proceedings, so when one of our number got up to go to his tent and walked, with a silly smile on his face, fully-dressed into the Thames, we were unable—incapable is perhaps the word—to come up with any conclusive findings. As for the hangover, we all agreed in the early morning that we felt remarkably fit. There were even occasional cries of "Yippee!" which suggested that the hangover, so far from departing silently, had not yet arrived.

Picnicking is, alas, not what it used to be. It's all very well to curl the lip as you roar on your way to some comfy roadhouse past the typical British family eating and enjoying the fresh fumes by the roadside. It could well be me and my lot, fully equipped with everything from matches and kindling wood to gas cooker and portable wine cooler, warding off starvation after five hours fruitless search in, say, Dorset or Cambridgeshire or the New Forest or even Windsor Great Park of blessed memory for just a few square feet of open, non-barbed-wired, non-hedged, non-gated-and-padlocked country in which to commune with nature and fry a banger. It was all right for Jane Austen and the Brontës and the rest of them—with a stroke of the pen they could have their characters owning half the countryside. As far as I'm concerned they still do.

I take it out once a year on the mountains of Wales (Scotland or the remoter Lake District would do as well) where, a few hundred feet above sea level, the loose stone walls peter out and you can roam at will with no one but sheep to watch your absurd goings-on. As for the future, it lies perhaps in communal picnicking in the old tradition. Already we have the Picnic Areas designated for it. The Germans, one stage ahead and bowing presumably to what they deem to be the inevitable, have for some years been furnishing their laybys with wooden tables and benches, all ready for communal sausage-slicing, *Stein*-tipping and martial song-singing.

Personally, if there is one square inch of this green and pleasant land still showing through the tarmac, I shall be there, charring it black.

"Open the window, Frisby, and shout yoo-hoo."

The Elegant Myope

THIS season, spectacles can be just as silly as hats, and that is saying something. The elegant myope who needs to wear glasses all the time does not make a virtue out of her necessity, she makes a vanity of it. In the delicate art of putting oneself over, spectacles have become a very important accessory.

Men, of course, have always made use of them in the architecture of character-building. In China they were regarded as a symbol of wisdom, a mark of degree; many a wise, clear-sighted mandarin had plain glass in his great round bamboo frames. Leather framed spectacles tied to the ears with strings were the sign of a man of substance in seventeenth-century Spain. In more modern times, in the nineteen-twenties, no American who wished "to win friends and influence people" could afford to be without horn-rimmed glasses, however keen his sight. Horn-rims did to the meaningless face what beards do to receding chins; in a world of dominoes, it was the double-blanks who wore the thickest, boldest rims.

Feminine vanity, on the other hand, does not lie so much in trying to impress with prosperity and success as to bowl over with beauty, grace, and charm. There are no early records of women wearing spectacles. Through the centuries ladies have worked in dim-lit castles at their interminable tapestries, in country houses at their unnecessary needlework and still less necessary water-colours, all without benefit of glasses. No urban society lady would admit to any weakness of sight. While men of fashion found the quizzer and the spy-glass telling elegancies, all that the lady of fashion could have was a little spy-glass hidden in her fan, or a magnifying glass in her scent bottle. Lorgnettes for ladies came later, for elderly ladies only.

Sun-glasses were the first spectacles to become accessories to the feminine mode. This was when it became the thing to go to the French Riviera in the dazzling summer instead of, as before, only in the paler sunshine of the winter months. Dark glasses, through this association, came to give an air of continental chic and idle richness. But to understand just why dark glasses aid attractiveness whereas clear glasses are a handicap to be overcome, it is necessary to recall the masked face at a ball: it is the mystery behind the mask, it is the glamour behind the dark lenses. For the wearer, it is also the sensation of being able to gaze unabashed, of being gazed at unembarrassed; it is boldness with the blinds drawn.

Everyday spectacles are just as highly-charged as sun-glasses: shaped as swans, trimmed with love-birds, some with earrings hanging from their side-pieces, the day of decadence is at hand. Upswept, harlequin, grasshopper, elfin . . . is it not time to call a halt? Time, indeed, to cry mercy! Yet the cumulative effect is such that even she who most genuinely wishes to contract out of the glamour game begins to feel dissatisfied with her exciting glasses. They look old-fashioned, they smack of National Health. A new pair, she thinks, would do more for her than a new hat; her new hat will do nothing for her without new glasses. She may prefer the new wavy side-pieces which are less severe than ordinary straight legs. If she wishes she can have glasses designed to her hair-style or a hair-style designed to her glasses. She must, there's no help for it, have several different pairs for different social occasions.

For evening, spectacles have turned into conversation pieces. Studded with coloured stones or diamanté, the best are the work of jewellers' craftsmen and can be matched to earrings and necklace. Diamanté clip-lorgnettes, however, have the greatest evening elegance, entirely free from the taint of necessity. These fold in two to form a dress clip, the back of the clip being the handle of the lorgnette. Less expensive folding lorgnettes are made in tortoise-shell, and sometimes coloured plastics. So modish, indeed, have lorgnettes become that one optician is extending the vogue still further back and introducing copies of eighteenth-century spy-glasses: first-rate accessories for First Nights.

Lorgnette gestures, carefully studied, can be effectively employed with spectacles proper; and an aid to such pretty by-play is the "Speclet" chain. This is a gilt chain which clips to the end of each side-piece and goes round the back of the neck. Primarily for public speakers who need spectacles for glancing at their notes, it is quite a thing for anyone who frequently takes her glasses off and on: and everyone *should*. For the art of wearing spectacles effectively, femininely, is not to let them be a static feature of the face. Taken off and on, swung on the hand, used for the pensive stroking of the chin, the absent-minded tapping of the teeth, the doodle on the table-cloth, spectacles are an instrument of flirtation as was the Edwardian fan. Only imagine! When sitting *tête-à-tête* there is the playful tap on the partner's shirt-front with the dainty jewel-studded glasses . . . followed by a blushing retreat behind the lenses till the music starts again.

ALISON ADBURGHAM

All restrictions on entertainment in Falkirk public bars are to be lifted for the next three months until new by-laws are drawn up, the magistrates decided yesterday at a special meeting. The action followed a complaint last week by Mr. William Fenney, the Provost, who said a go-go dancer, dressed in a bikini, put his spectacles inside her panties. *(Glasgow Herald)*

My Old Man's a Trencherman

MICHAEL PARKINSON

LIFE is a boring business and made more so by those people who preach moderation in all things. They are a mournful lot and more of them live on this island than anywhere else. The British are experts at doing everything in moderation, which accounts for our licensing laws, our hotels which serve dinner between seven pm and eight fifteen pm, and the fact that Britons are lousy lovers. What is more we prop up this dreary embargo on our natural impulses by repeating the old lie that self-denial is a virtue.

Our attitude to food and drink is that a little of both at the right time of day is all right, but too much of either is disgusting and a certain indication of a wrong 'un. We are one of the few tribes on this planet that does not regard eating as an occasion to be savoured with the eyes, the nose and the palate as well as the belly. We eat and drink without joy and we only eat and drink because if we didn't we would die.

There are exceptions and my old man was one of them. It is from him that I inherited my remarkable capacity for consuming and enjoying large quantities of both food and drink. His confrontation with the meal that was set in front of him on his return from a shift down the pit was a ritual which never varied in all the years that I lived at home. First he would have Yorkshire pudding, not one of those cissy little jobs that look like tennis balls but a proper man-sized one made in a huge meat dish and light and fluffy as thistledown. This pudding would be swamped with a gallon of gravy and downed for starters. He would follow this with a mountain of mashed potatoes, a ton of greens, a turnip or two and half a cow. As a sweet course he would eat a large pie dish full of rice pudding and would round off the occasion with another man-sized Yorkshire pudding which he covered in strawberry jam.

His face at the end of his meal was a picture of sublime satisfaction and it stayed that way as he fell asleep in his chair by the fire while his digestive system went to work. He loved eating and demanded of anyone at his table that they shared his enjoyment. He could not abide people who were choosy about their food and he hated waste. Even a morsel left on a plate was enough for him to institute an inquiry about the state of the person's bowels and would inevitably end with him administering the castor oil.

I could never match his appetite although I often tried. It was always the Yorkshire pudding with jam on it that beat me. Then I left home and went in the army and lived on

NAAFI chips and Mars bars. My first leave was only a forty-eight-hour pass but I hitch-hiked all the way from Wiltshire to Yorkshire just to get some decent grub. I sat with father at the table and the ritual began. First the Yorkshire pudding swamped in gravy, then the spuds and turnips and cabbage and beef. Then the rice pudding. The old man watched me critically as I went at the Yorkshire pudding and the strawberry jam. I downed it in a second. Just to crown my triumph I ended up by devouring half a loaf and a tin of treacle. "Finished?" said the old man, eventually. I nodded. "Army's done thi' good lad. Improved thi' appetite. Tha' should sign on I'm thinking," he said. Then he took me to the pub. It was the first time he had ever asked me to accompany him to the boozer and it was his tribute from one big eater to another.

I have never forgotten that day nor that meal. I have never improved on the performance although I did come close to it once in one of those help yourself joints in London when I had the manager hovering anxiously as I carved a fifth helping from the beef. In case you are wondering what the Parkinsons are shaped like I might tell you that I look like a yard of wet string and my old man has never weighed more than twelve stone. Never mind what the killjoys tell you, me and my old man are living proof that gluttony is good for you.

"Can you recommend a medium dry champagne suitable for launching a ship of twenty thousand tons?"

Five Star Hotel

SLIM as a splinter,
   stern, parental,
Frankfurt's Inter-
   continental,

a new hotel,
   from the skyline soars,
a sentinel
   on thirty floors.

its shoulders break
   the clouds apart,
a concrete stake
   in the city's heart:

a paradise
   for the well-heeled guest:
at a topmost price
   he gets the best:

lounges manned
   by instant waiters,
music (canned)
   in the elevators:

"For a time Brother Sebastian was exposed to the follies of the world outside."

masses of headroom
  everywhere
and in the bedroom
  space to spare:

a bathroom fitted
  with four main "pieces,"
shelves well kitted,
  towels like fleeces:

two Bibles at
  my *bedde's hedde,*
pristine, fat,
  discreetly ready

to fit me for
  sleep or a sermon
in English or,
  if German, German:

bedlights graded
  to choice of pitch
(strong, soft, shaded)
  with pillow switch:

and if none's the right light,
  a half-inch thick
white wax nightlight
  with unused wick.

*   *   *

These quenched, to You
  I make a prayer,
*Dominus illu-
  minatio mea.*

RICHARD USBORNE

A man questioned by a gamekeeper pulled four brown trout from the swimming trunks he was wearing, Bowland magistrates were told.   *(Blackburn Star)*

The Beautiful People

WILLIAM DAVIS

IT is difficult, these days, to open a magazine or newspaper without finding advice on how to lose weight, get fit, look beautiful, and generally prepare to meet The Challenge of the Summer.

Most of the seasonal propaganda starts with the request that you "take a long cool look at yourself in the mirror," and assumes that you won't like what you see. I am not sure this is really justified; to the starry-eyed everything is beautiful. But let us accept, for the moment, that your long cool look does indeed reveal one or two minor imperfections. What should you do about it?

My own first step—and I speak as someone with considerable experience—is to sit down in my most comfortable chair and have a large Scotch. Don't believe what the medical books tell you about the therapeutic value of tea; Scotch is infinitely more effective in the treatment of shock.

My second step is to have another Scotch.

My third step is to resolve that something must be done—tomorrow.

My fourth step is to reach for a book I bought for these occasions. It's by Sir Francis Chichester, and it is charmingly entitled "How to keep fit, by one who never is as fit as he would like to be". It rarely fails to inspire me. I cannot claim that it has made me any fitter, but just reading it fills me with determination and makes me feel that, at last, I have made a start. "I would like," Sir Francis declares, "to be as fit as a tiger in the prime of life. I don't mean that I want to be able to carry a full-size bullock in my jaws without it touching the ground for four miles, but I would like to have a tiger's agility, endurance, speed, sight and hearing, and, perhaps I might add, its grace of movement". *My sentiments precisely!*

Sir Francis, it seems, has a half hour of glory every morning—a period which, he says, "can best be likened to the stretching, arching, and yawning of a cat or dog on awakening". I find the yawning part easier than the stretching and arching, but I have tried the lot. Oh yes, I have. It's not so bad, really, once you get used to it. I should, however, warn you of one little snag. It makes me very hungry. I suspect it happens to tigers too—but they don't have to take long cool looks at themselves in the mirror.

Sir Francis copes with this by using a thing called a Guelpa. No, settle down, it's a diet. Well, not so much a diet as a torture. Named after the Italian who developed it, the Guelpa forces you to have nothing but apple juice on the first day, and nothing but very dry toast on the second. You won't, of course, have any energy left for stretching and arching, and Sir

Francis kindly points out one or two other results; he becomes intolerant and impatient, flies into a temper if thwarted or held up, or rushes into doing something rash when he ought to be thinking. But you do feel fitter at the end of it, and if you lose your job and life companion in the meantime, well—nothing in this world is perfect.

I lack Sir Francis's courage, so the Guelpa is out. I have looked at other diets, but I confess that I find this whole dieting business very confusing. No two experts ever seem to agree. One tells you to eat nothing but fat: another insists this is the quickest way to become a seventeen stone weakling. A third urges you to drop everything except potatoes; a fourth maintains with complete conviction, that if you do anything so stupid you might as well start saving for your funeral. One's colleagues are no help either. One claims that he's lost six pounds by giving up fruit; another says that he's lost six pounds by eating nothing but fruit. And what, pray, is one to make of the cookery book, just published, which lists the favourite recipes of fifty of London's top models? What these delectable ladies like best, it seems, are rich, fattening things like sausage and tomato pie (Jean Shrimpton), apple crumble (Sue Murray), tagliatelli (Maria Landi) and vegetable pasties (Patti Boyd).

Like most people, I am a sucker for anything which promises to make one slim and beautiful without effort. The *Daily Mirror* has been running a "diet plan" which does just that. "Cheer up," the paper announced on the first day, "you can do the whole job painlessly—well, almost—in a week".

Step one looked intriguing. "On waking, have a small tumbler of water at room temperature, then lie back for five minutes before getting up. This helps to start the kidneys working—very good for weight loss!" I tried it, and indeed went one better. I lay back for fifteen minutes. I haven't lost any weight yet, but that may just possibly have something to do with the fact that a couple of gin and tonics were forced on me before lunch. That's another thing with diets: friends see it as some kind of challenge. The moment you announce that you're on a diet everyone tries to get you off it. "Oh, come on," they insist "a little drink can't do you any harm".

The *Mirror* has also been carrying some of those small ads which claim that you can lose ten pounds in ten days by going on a Grapefruit Diet. "This diet," it says, "lets you eat normally, and you can include forbidden foods, such as steaks trimmed with fats, sausages and scrambled eggs, and still lose weight". That's the kind of positive talk I like to hear.

A trim young thing I know has a method which, according to her, is even more effective. She goes to restaurants as usual, but orders only food which she detests. She cannot, for example, stand the sight of liver. So that's what she asks for every night for a whole week; with temptation thus eliminated, she has no difficulty losing weight.

My own favourite is a diet which I developed after reading, oddly enough, a little book called "how to put *on* weight". I call it the "worry diet," and it is based on a very simple principle. According to the author of the book, Dr. Robert Andrew, worry is one of the chief causes of underweight. People who are skinny—he prefers the word "slender"—tend to spend an awful lot of time worrying themselves sick about all sorts of problems which fatties merely laugh at. They are, as the good doctor puts it "all twitched up". Ergo, if worry keeps slender people from putting on weight, it should also help those who are . . . er . . . well-built to shed a few surplus inches.

The trouble is, of course, that you can measure food and drink in terms of calories, but not worry. You know the impact of, say, a pork chop or a gin and tonic, but not that of a night spent wide awake, worrying over a bank manager's letter or an important business decision. But this is easily remedied. After much study I have drawn up the following basic chart. It is intended purely for guidance; you will naturally want to compile one of your own.

1. Will it rain tomorrow? A good, solid, fundamental worry . . .

50 CALORIES

2. My God, I didn't really say all that last night, did I? An effective early morning worry . . .

65 CALORIES

3. Who's that new chap in the office? . . .

84 CALORIES

4. What did the chairman mean by that remark? . . .

73 CALORIES

5. Is that a police car just behind me? . . .

33 CALORIES

6. I'm putting on too much weight . . .

90 CALORIES

I am sure you will be able to think of many more: if you really try, there's no end to the things you can worry about.

Diets, of course, are only part of the struggle. Sir Francis's views on the value of stretching and arching are shared by an extraordinarily large number of people. *Vogue* this month urges its readers to "take a long cool look at yourself in the mirror," and goes on to state, flatly, that "now is the time to start body gardening". London, it seems, is full of gardeners determined to peel skins, tone muscles, wax legs, and do all sorts of incredible things with thighs and stomachs. There are places which will "cultivate a swan-like neck" and others which will give you "delicate hands and feet". Most of these torture chambers are dedicated to women, but there are also a very large number of gyms—and beauty salons—catering for every male mood, from spartan to near luxury.

Yoga seems to be increasingly popular. It brings me back, somewhat reluctantly, to Sir Francis and his tiger envy. "I believe," he declares, "that Yoga is, taken as a whole, the best system of exercising". He goes on to list a few favourites. The section I like best is headed "relaxing," and I'm sure he won't mind if I give you a brief sample: "Run your thoughts over your joints and muscles, to check that they are all relaxed and free from any tension. It will help if you review in turn toe joints, ankles, leg muscles, knees, thighs, hips—all these first for one leg then the other. Then think of all the vertebrae in your spine, starting from the tail and ending at the neck . . ."

Need I go on? What are you waiting for? Don't you want to be beautiful?

BACHELOR CHAMBERS

(By one in search of the perfect hermitage)

MY tastes are modest and my needs are small:—
Three bright and lofty chambers (parquet floor),
Each thirty feet or so by twenty-four,
With bathroom (entered from an airy hall)
  Where hot and cold habitually run;
  And such a set of aspects that the sun
Leaves me in light the whole day long. That's all.

They must be central—somewhere like Pall Mall;
  In touch with London's throbbing heart, or hub,
  And fairly near the Athenaeum Club
And restaurants; yet silent as a well,
  For here no taxi-hooters must intrude
  To jar upon the meditative mood
Or operate against the Muse's spell.

For service—just one handmaid, nice and neat;
  A valet, soft of foot; a chef of wits
  For homely dinners based upon the Ritz;
And, at his post abutting on the street,
  A liveried page to brush me for the Park,
  Vigilant of my wants, yet slow to mark
What ladies most affect my fair retreat.

The outlook (need I add?) should be on trees;
  And for inclusive rent I'd gladly pay
  Full Garden City prices. I should say
There must be many men with tastes like these
  All round St. James's—men without a wife
  And wedded solely to the Simple Life;
And yet the agents find me hard to please!

O.S.

Weekend at the *TOP*

LORD ARRAN
on Huntin', Shootin', and Spongin'

I SUPPOSE I have been to nearly a thousand weekend parties during my life. Nowadays, alas, the invitations are tending to drop off. One becomes less of a social asset as one grows older. "Boofy," I can hear my friends say, "is too slow and too deaf. And he's become rather messy with his food."

I should explain incidentally that I was brought up never to use the word "weekend" and I do so now with some distaste. My parents regarded it as very vulgar; and indeed I still avoid it when I remember to. The phrase was "Saturday to Monday" or "Friday to Monday" if one was shooting on Saturday.

But then the shibboleths are dying out. My aunts never asked for one's address. What is your "direction," they would say. This to the uninitiated was misleading. "North-east by east," they would reply, or "I am a director of several companies." *I* say—God help me—"address."

Yes, I bow to the times and accept that the word "weekend" is now widely used, even by the French among whom it is apparently the smart thing to talk English among themselves—"'Ow you getting along, Baby?''

"Top class, and you?"

To me the weekend party is the most marvellous thing in the world. If I am good, God will reward me with an unending series of them.

The excitement of arrival, the same excitement of forty years back. The question of who else will be there. Some hostesses tell you in advance, some don't. On three occasions I have had to leave at once because I found myself confronted by my worst enemy: why do one's friends so often like one's enemies—such bad taste. The whispered conversation with one's wife "Oh God, those boring Brigstocks again!" Or perhaps, usually in fact, the people one loves most. The kiss of affectionate salutation; then the large cold gin-and-tonic to take to one's bedroom and drink in one's hot bath. Tomorrow we shall do nothing, just talk and eat, particularly talk—often brilliant talk—with perhaps a little walk round the garden. This surely is what life is all about.

But of course, though still much the same in many ways, the weekend has changed like everything else. Today most prople arrive by motor-car. In 1930 one was told which train to catch. From Wilton one received a printed card with the time of one's own train, 4.30 ("Servants and luggage by the 3.30" to enable them of course to have unpacked for one in advance). Today quite often we pack and unpack for ourselves. Imagine! And tipping; before the war thirty bob was overtipping; double it now and you're never asked again because it gets back from the housemaid to the hostess that you're an old meanie.

Weekend Investment

And if there's a big shoot on the Saturday, it costs about £30 all in, what with tips to loaders and keepers and cartridges at sevenpence a bang. True, you save the cost of the gas and the booze and the roast beef you would have had at home. But gracious living even at other people's expense sets one back quite a bit. And what it costs one's hosts! To be vulgar and talk about money, I reckon we have cost them more than £20,000 in all since we married. May I—and this is quite serious—thank them from a full heart for their kindness and generosity, more especially as we don't entertain them, or very rarely, in our own suburban villa chiefly because we can't hope to keep up with their standards.

And these standards are immensely high; higher by far than before the war. The comfort and luxury are greater—it is rare for each bedroom not to have its own bathroom; the food, always the best in the world and better than any Parisian restaurant, has now reached new heights, though of course there is less of it. Gone, thank God, those six-course dinners; in their place two or three.

Wine, Women and Naked Butlers

The drink flows: in most houses there is a grog tray in the drawing room all day and all night so that one can give oneself a drink whenever one wants to. Personally I would never help myself without asking my host or hostess first, but many people do. Bad manners, I would say. Champagne before or after dinner or both. Claret or white Burgundy over the nosh. No one ever gets drunk though sometimes someone becomes a little argumentative.

Only in the matter of domestic servants has there been a change downwards. Three or four now do the work of thirteen or fourteen plus the hostess herself active behind the scenes. What the other ten used to do heaven only knows. To me they are epitomised by Hilaire Belloc's "the man who cleans the Billiard-room."

The women's clothes too are much simpler, though probably just as expensive if not more so. Short pretty frocks in the evenings, and gosh they look nice! No one ever wears what I believe is called a *robe de style*. True, I once stayed in the same house as a Countess—and being an Earl I am in favour of Countesses on principle—who changed five times in one day. But perhaps she just liked to feel nice and fresh.

I must admit the young men's clothes are a bit way out, though even I wear a frilly shirt and a blue velvet bow tie in the evenings, and very nice I look too. And after all it is only twenty years since the door was opened to a twenty-year-old girl relation of mine by a stark naked butler and received by an equally stark naked host, a defunct press lord. Being well brought up and capable of dealing with any situation, however unconventional, she remained as cool as a cucumber though not to the extent of taking off her own clothes. I think his Lordship was a little surprised and put out by her sang-froid, though it was almost certainly the first naked man she had ever seen in her life.

What next? Love. Sometimes it plays its part in the week-ends we go to, but never noticeably, although my wife says I never notice *anything*. And I suppose it does go under my nose, licit and illicit: but I prefer not to know. Engaged or newly married couples seldom get asked because they are tiresome and embarrassing. Of course when I was young the first thing I did on arriving was to look for the prettiest bird in the party and try to have—again—what one of my aunts would call a "spangle". And as many of the parties of those days consisted of twenty or even thirty people, there was plenty of choice.

In my father's day, there was widespread, illicit romance at country-house parties, or so he told me. This was indeed connived at and even contrived by the most respectable hostesses in the greatest country-houses who would say to the housekeeper when arranging where the visitors were to sleep, "I think we will put Lord X in the Chinese room and let me see now—yes, and Mrs. Y in the Chippendale room" (the two rooms happened of course to be next door to one another). And on Sunday morning the whole party would go to church, including of course the couple who had spent the night naked in each other's arms (I seem to have nakedness on the brain). But I do not propose to start writing about Edwardian hypocrisy, though there was much to be said for it.

So much for indoor games, now for sport. Hunting weekends are rare: but then I don't hunt, though my wife does. Most people hunt from home. Shooting is the biggest "occasion" if not the cause for weekend parties nowadays, and if you don't shoot, you miss a lot of parties. I am thinking of giving it up because having been a decent second-class shot, I can't hit a thing. But my wife begs me not to—"If you do, we shan't be asked anywhere," she says—and correctly. "But shooting as I am, we probably won't be asked anyway," I say, though I am not sure. People nowadays, with some notable exceptions, ask you for your company and not your skill.

Sometimes shooting does not follow the conventional pattern. One of my most loyal hosts has the habit of bringing out with him some of the larger carnivores. First it was a leopard, which used to retrieve or alternatively eat the dead birds. It used also to scare poachers into fits. Next it was a lion, which eventually savaged its trainer. Last an even more ferocious animal. This was the cause of some embarrassment to me. While enjoying a quiet kip in bed after shooting, I heard a scuffling outside and the door noiselessly opened to be shut immediately. I switched on the light. Facing me was a large Bengal tiger. It was growling. I kept my head, I said "Nice tigey, good tigey! Tigey, tigey, tigey!" More growls, and gales of giggles from outside. I drew all the sheets over me and waited for death. The tiger started scratching itself. After a while its owner opened the door. This year, if I am invited, I confidently expect a boa-constrictor.

But this is summer; what can we expect? Tennis and golf, of course, and almost invariably a big swimming-pool—occasionally an indoor pool, where the weather doesn't count. People coming over for drinks or luncheon, and "I really must see Hidcote this afternoon," or "Fairford is only twenty miles away. I want to see the glass."—"No. Let's do bloody nothing." And so we do bloody nothing, and we sleep and talk a bit and read the Sunday papers. And soon it is drinky time again. And after dinner most of us go home. Tomorrow we must work.

As we grow older and tend to spit and rumble internally, I deeply hope we may still receive the occasional letter beginning "Dear Fiona and Boofy, We wondered whether you could come to us for the weekend of September 28. Do try." And we shall feel wanted and know that two days at least of sheer joy lie ahead.

Girl (to young man who has asked for a second cherry in his cocktail). *"What's the great idea, Tony?"*
Tony. *"Family medical adviser insists I must eat more fruit."*

Make Fat Not War
Says WILLIAM HARDCASTLE

I GIVE you this slogan for the 'seventies. I will grant you that, though he couldn't see his jackboots except in the mirror, Herman Goering wasn't exactly what you would call cuddly. Sidney Greenstreet showed that girth and gruesomeness can be menacingly combined. Yet I am convinced that the world would be a better place if we all proceeded to unloosen our girdles and make these the non-slimming 'seventies. Let calories be unconfined.

I must declare, as they say, an interest. I have been chubby since an early age. I was known on the block as the boy with his shirt tail always hanging out; the shape of my bottom had some curious unsettling effect on my underwear. Since then I have never looked back. Over the years I have managed to tame my shirt tails, but otherwise I remain, as they say in the more polite men's shops, portly.

I have achieved this against constant and excessive brainwashing and propaganda. Another such exercise is being mounted at this moment. As regularly as Christmas trees shed their pine needles, the Dames of Fleet Street give up their space around this time of year to post-holiday slimming diets. They assume their readers have blown themselves up over the past few weeks and conceive it as their duty to help them deflate.

It isn't as if they ever had anything new to say. They just get out the old cuttings and switch things round a bit—two leaves of lettuce, instead of three of spinach, for Wednesday lunch, and so on. As if, to any intelligent person, such advice was necessary. Anybody knows how to get thin—you just stop eating and drinking. But *why*?

When Mae West said, "Come Up and See Me Sometime," one knew that, if one did go up, there would be plenty to see. I'm delighted to note that that splendid lady is operating to this day on the principle that you can't have enough of a good thing. By contrast the poor brain-washed modern girl's main aim is to become the nearest thing to a blood-drained corpse this side of the municipal mortuary. Her partner's desire is for his ribs to be seen pushing through his unisex blouse. This benighted couple are flying in the face not only of Miss Mae West but also of historical fact. This has established beyond peradventure that to be fat is to be content and jovial.

There are, as I have said, exceptions to this rule. Benito Mussolini and Nikita Khrushchev were both broad of beam but neither can be said to have been plumply endearing. But take Winston Churchill—never a man to neglect his mutton chops, his champagne or his brandy.

I am glad to see that both the main political leaders in Britain today have a tendency towards avoirdupois. Edward Heath may have been unloading ballast lately in pursuit of his East of Suez (or West of Tasmania) policy. But I can't help feeling that he shares a similar metabolism with Harold Wilson, and that both have a built-in leaning towards corpulence. Only poor Jeremy Thorpe maintains a fashionable cadaverousness, a fact which, I feel sure, bodes no good for the Liberals at the forthcoming elections.

The main argument against fatness, of course, is that it is bad for your health and leads to an early grave. You will get this information from doctors who, as any underwriter will tell you, are among the worst risks that ever gave the Man from the Prudential a sleepless night. If you'd taken the doctors' advice a few years ago you would have laid off sugar and been swilling cyclamates day and night. Now where would you be? The fact is that in modern life there is danger in everything, and one of the dangers which, in my view, is not sufficiently stressed is that involved in dieting.

To summarise briefly, it can ruin your business career, destroy your marriage, and send your children cowering into a corner. This is because dieting makes you bad-tempered. It is the happily plump peddler who pulls off the big sale. The well-fed spouse keeps the home fires burning. It is the hungry father who snarls at his offspring. And I speak only of the domestic scene. On the wider stage it has been as often as not, the haggard scarecrow-like statesman who has earned most of history's demerits. Rather than rush out and pick a fight, the portly politico is much more likely to put his feet up and doze a bit while matters simmer down.

In all charity I should say that incurably thin people deserve our sympathy. I once had the bright idea of running a get-fat diet in a paper I was editing and instructed a woman writer (I think, as a matter of fact, it was Olga Franklin) to map it out. We ran groaning menus every day for a fortnight, but the result was a total flop. As I say, getting thin is easy; you just put the stopper back on the light ale and confine your intake to small lean steaks and lettuce (with no olive oil in the dressing). But to get fat is a blessing that is forever denied to some.

There's a fellow in my office who you can practically see through. Every day he has three buttered buns for elevenses. Yet he still looks like an advanced case of kwashiorkor. To somebody like him, one's heart goes out. But that is no reason why Betty Banting of the *Sunday Excess* should try and get us all to look the same.

Aesthetic arguments are used in support of slimming, and truthfulness compels me to admit that the picture which accompanies this article is a fairly accurate one. But Rubens wouldn't have picked me for a model, anyway. There were plenty of nice fat models around, without bothering about the obviously imperfect ones. What, I ask you, would Rubens have done with Twiggy? One can almost see the palette being flung in anger across the studio.

No, other explanations for the slimming craze must be sought and they could prove to be ominous. One theory is that it is a plot by the international airlines who are seeking to breed, like so many battery farmers, a narrow buttocked species. This way they can cram more emaciated human beings into their wretched aeroplanes. I must say that whenever I step into a modern jet I feel I'm breaking some supranational aviation agreement, and causing a remote computer to flinch.

There is also, of course, a slimming industry. On distant Welsh trading estates production lines churn out pseudo-foods which are guaranteed to nauseate and not to inflate. Whole counters in chemists' shops are now devoted to such commodities, and the price of starving comes high. Electronic engineers have developed pulsing belts which wrapped around a distended waistline allegedly rub off the inches without effort. There are salons and societies and a whole library of literature, equally dedicated to the concave stomach and the protruding collar bone. All this apart from the wit's-end woman's editor who can't think of a damn thing to write about in the weeks after Christmas.

But, in truth, the conspiracy theory doesn't really stand up. The craze is just that—a passing psychological hula-hoop, a game of yo-yo with the body cells. It is time we were done with such childish things.

We have all been instructed lately by press, television and radio of the errors we communally committed in the 'sixties. Only shortage of space and air time can explain their omission of the subject I now bring to your attention. I would like everybody (to coin a phrase) to put their weight behind it. Make fat, not war. Or, to put it another way, Think Big.

"That remark was in exquisitely bad taste."

BARBECUE

"We're not early, are we?"

"Takes you right back to the Western Desert, doesn't it?"

"I say, you haven't got the mustard in here, have you?"

"Could Eunice have hers well done?"

When a Young Man's Fancy...

MY son fell in love again last month. This happens two or three times a year. He usually says This Time it is Different. He has gone a step further and says This Time it is the Real Thing.

We like him being in love. It means we hardly see him. He is quiet at breakfast, goes off to his studies all day, returns for a quick tea, bath and change, and is off to meet Her forthwith. We seldom see him again before we retire. It also means he baths and shaves every day without being asked, cajoled, shouted at, implored, or as a last resort, ordered to do these small things.

We do not have to listen to his musical choice for evenings on end. This is either r. 'n' r. (lessening in its popularity, thank goodness, as his twenties approach) or solid harpsichord long play, which sounds a little tinny to our ears during the third hour.

Housekeeping accounts show a good credit for once. We can afford to entertain more during these periods. When the current love is brought home she never eats a hearty meal. She toys with morsels, the while she gazes at my male offspring, obviously longing to get away from the rest of us.

I remember my first words on seeing him nearly twenty years ago. I said "He's just like a pug". The rugged, pug-faced lad appears to be more handsome than we thought. Indeed, my daughter, after careful study to discover what They see in her brother, has reported that by candlelight he is quite glam.

Alas! The path of love, true or otherwise, never runs smooth.

The first, or Introductory-Probation Phase, is the best for all concerned. It is then we have the eagerness to please, the urge for outer cleanliness, the pressing (by himself) of suitings, Bedfords, jackets, ties, scarves. The charm is practised on us at home, to ensure perfection in action. No more the surly grunts, the voracious animal rushing through dinner with revolting noise, tearing off when the last mouthful is downed, unless it is a dreaded evening in, with music. The precious motor-bike can rust. Only urgent repairs are carried out, so that oily rags, filthy tools, tyres, what-have-yous are not brought into his room for overhaul.

This phase is too short for us, even if it is prolonged for eight weeks.

Phase Two is soon with us. This lasts the longest. It is the seeing every day, staying up late, talking or dancing or dining every night time. Too tired every morning, sleepy, grumpy, late up, late for breakfast, late leaving home. He has to be called half a dozen times at least before he even hears.

This might be termed the Panic Phase, for the rest of the family. We all begin to think it might be serious. We worry. But presently the first ominous sign appears. There is a request one Thursday "Could you lend me five bob, please?" The next week it is a request for £1 on the Tuesday. He is getting broke. The testing time has come.

No sensible, normal young man in his late teens likes to be penniless. The battle, Woman versus Solvency, is on. Phase Three is here. The Painless Disposal.

There are long and earnest talks with each of us. He examines the situation from every angle. It is foolish in the extreme to marry young, while one is still studying. He announces what we all knew. He has been seeing too much of her. He is not "at home" when she phones. We refuse to lie to the poor, unhappy nearly ex-love, so he dashes out of the front door like a frightened stag when he hears the telephone. As we receive a lot of calls during an average evening, he may do this five or six times before the expected call arrives. My husband, who has often waited fifteen minutes or longer for the heir to our overdrafts when they are going out together, is always amazed at his speed.

Doubt, certainty, contrition and other emotions hold sway for a few days each. At last Phase Three is over. My son breathes a great sigh of relief, rings up all his male friends and goes out on parties unencumbered by women. He says what we all know "It's wonderful to be free"

But is it?

DIANA CHILDE

"I do believe you're right—'47—an excellent year."

49

Goon for Lunch
Back at Ten

HARRY SECOMBE

THE phone rang at home. "How would you like to go to the finest restaurant in France for lunch and come back the same day, all expenses paid?" asked William Davis. "Just give me five minutes to pack my knife, fork and spoon," I said.

And so Harry Secombe, the oldest cub reporter in the world, boarded an Air France plane at 9.20 in the morning bound for Lyons and La Pyramide Restaurant, one of the few in France to which Michelin gives three stars and which resounds to the refined chomping of the most expensive choppers in the whole of Europe.

Sitting back in my seat, I allowed myself a brief reverie of memorable meals I had partaken of in the past. I remembered the bread pudding we used to have for afters in the army in Aldershot in 1941. Our new Sergeant Cook vowed that we would have bread pudding at every meal until we stopped wasting bread. I began to acquire a taste for it and as the weeks went by I wasted so much bread that I was put on a charge.

I remembered a summer's night in Bert's Cafe near the Slips, Swansea, where I proposed to Myra over tea and slightly stale doughnuts. I had three to her one, saying "Marry me and one day we will be eating champagne and caviar". "That's right, love," she said without conviction as she paid the bill.

Upon reflection I began to wonder if I was the right man for the job. Head waiters, particularly on the continent, single me out for special inattention. Just as a horse knows immediately and instinctively when its rider is an idiot, so a head waiter greets my entrance to a restaurant with a knowing aside to his assistants, "Nous avons a right one here".

He usually lets me simmer at the table until I begin to believe the story of the head waiter who died and had inscribed on his tombstone "At last God caught his eye". Then when I am considered to be just about on the boil he comes along and whisks me with the menu, stirring briskly, talks fast kitchen Italian to taste, until my mind approaches the consistency of smooth paste and I find myself ordering the most expensive dish he has to offer, which upon close inspection turns out to be a kind of rissole.

On arrival, a car complete with young chauffeur awaited me. "Aah, la puissance de Punch," I exclaimed. He smiled incomprehendingly. After a few miles my stock French phrases ran out. "Meubles," I said desperately as we passed a furniture shop. "Oui," he said, vaguely surprised. A quarter of a mile of silence later I said "Boulangerie". He nodded uncomfortably.

"Have you got any caviar?"

After I had idiotically pointed out a hospital, a paper shop and a funeral parlour he said "I learn English. If Monsieur would like to speak with me it would be good for my study." I accepted with relief. "Blimey, I felt a right twit," I said. He looked uncomfortable. We rode on in silence. Then, "Pharmacy," he said, indicating a chemist shop.

The drive out to Vienne, where the restaurant is situated, takes about 45 minutes. The weather was sunny and I watched the glorious scenery flash past with a mounting feeling of excitement. It seemed no time before we arrived at Vienne, which is a very ancient town where Pontius Pilate is supposed to have ended his days. From what I saw of it, it was much too good for him.

We came at last to my gastronomic mecca as we rounded the four-fronted arch surmounted by a pyramid from which the restaurant takes its name. Founded in 1920 by Monsieur Fernand Point, it has become over the years a place of pilgrimage for the world's top gourmets.

The restaurant garden was green and lovely, but with one unusual feature, there were empty bottles stuck all over the fruit trees. This perplexed me somewhat. Inside the restaurant a young waiter wearing a long white apron seemed to know that I was the gentleman from England. There was an atmosphere of deceptive homely provincial charm about the place. The room had a low ceiling with wood panelled walls, green velvet curtains at the windows, and three rows of tables ran its whole length. A large oval table stood before the wooden screen at the kitchen end of the restaurant. On it were rows of gleaming cutlery and a huge carved wooden bowl containing enough lemons for a whole football season of half time refreshments.

The place wasn't very full. The dress of the clientele was in the main casual, and although the chatter was relaxed and uninhibited, one could hear above everything the faint rustle of crisp 100 franc notes. This was obviously not luncheon voucher territory. But why, I asked myself, should they hang bottles on trees in the garden? I was placed at a table in the right hand corner of the room and as I sat down I took out a small note book and put it in front of me, determined to record this momentous meal course by course.

The head waiter was a short, red-faced, jolly little man who introduced himself as Monsieur Vincent and handed me a large menu before bustling away. On the front of the menu was the Pyramide motif which, incidentally, was repeated throughout the restaurant. Even the butter on each table was moulded in its shape. I viewed the menu with reverence and was faced with an agonising choice of classic French dishes written in longhand. I decided to let the Maitre D'Hotel choose for me. "Je suis dans vos mains," I said. He winced a little then smiled. "Permettez-moi, monsieur," was his reply as he whipped the menu away. Remembering my past experiences with head waiters I had a sudden vision of rissoles.

The long crusty bread roll looked very inviting and as I sank my teeth into it I made a note on my pad. "Long crusty bread roll," I wrote. The wine list arrived along with the wine waiter in a green baize apron. I mention them in that order because of the size of the wine list. It was enormous and rather than spend a long time holding it I asked the wine waiter to recommend a half bottle of white and a half bottle of red. He came back with an unlabelled white wine in a bucket. When I asked him the name I was unable to understand what he said, so not wanting to seem impolite I nodded sagely. "Vin blanc" I jotted on my pad.

"Brioche de foie gras," said the waiter as he laid the first course before me. I tabulated its description for posterity. "Square slice of sweet bread with round piece of pâté in the middle—very nice." I ate it quickly, not having had any breakfast. For no reason at all I worried again about the bottles on the trees.

Very soon the waiter was back with a second course. "Mousse de fruite périgueuse," he announced. I picked up my fork and spoon and demolished it in seconds. "Cylindrical shaped mousse with black gritty bits in the sauce" was my entry. I took a quick swill of wine and sat back sweating slightly. Monsieur Vincent came across to the table. "Mange doucement, monsieur," he admonished kindly. I had the grace to blush and resolved to treat the next course with more delicacy.

Turbot au champagne was almost immediately in front of me. The service throughout being prompt and impeccable. Now this was really delicious. Probably the best fish course I have ever tasted. I lingered over the sauce, surreptitiously dipping the remains of my roll in it and washing the whole lot down with great drafts of the white wine. "Smashing—not a bone in it," was my written comment.

The waiters then entered bearing a huge serving dish called, I believe, a *torpilleure*, on which were two smaller silver dishes and between them a bowl containing two roses. This course turned out to be *Caneton Nantais au Poire Vert*. It was duck cooked in a rich sauce with a side plate of thinly sliced potatoes done in a kind of omelette. The wine waiter brought along a bottle of Côte Rotie, 1964. He poured out a little for me to taste. I made a great business of rolling the wine around my tongue with my eyes shut. "A very good year for corks," I quipped. "Pardon, monsieur?" his eyes narrowed a little. "Très bien," I said hastily, starting to tackle the duck. I was beginning to breathe heavily by this time and although I ate the omelette I left some of the duck. The wine was having an effect on my notes too. "Duck" was all I managed to write, relying on my taste buds to be the espouser of lost courses.

Another glass of wine and along came the cheese. Excellent it was and to make sure of the name I got the waiter to put it down for me. "Coulommiers" was what he wrote. I hoped it wasn't a rude comment. The next courses are a little mixed in my mind. Did I really have *Gateau Marjolaine* followed by fresh strawberries and cream and a sorbet? There are traces on my waistcoat to prove that I must have.

My eyes were beginning to close as Monsieur Vincent approached with a bottle of liqueur containing a fully grown pear. He insisted that I should taste some with my coffee. I wondered vaguely how the pear got inside, until a very French looking couple at the next table, who turned out to be very English, explained how it was done. They put the neck of the bottle over a bud on the pear tree and let it grow inside, then when the pear is ripe they remove the bottle from the tree and fill it up with pear brandy. "Of course, how simple," I beamed around the room, replete and happy with the best meal I had ever had safely under my belt and the mystery solved. The bill came and went without removing the smile from my face and I insisted on shaking hands with all the staff. "Vive le Common Market," I said. "Oui," was the qualified reply.

I was still smiling when I got home at ten that night. "Well, was it worth the trip?" asked my wife, fresh from cooking beefburgers for the kids' supper. "Best meal I've ever had," I said. "In a restaurant that is," I added quickly seeing her expression. "Bet they couldn't make a proper cup of tea," she said placing one before me. "They certainly couldn't," I said, "but they can grow pears in bottles." "You've been drinking," she said.

HOW TO LIVE LONGER

ATTEND. I do not often sing to you
To make you healthier, but now I do.
The word coronary does not come down
From *cor*, the heart, but from *corona*, crown;
And I, for one, pronounce it in this way
Whatever medical young men may say.
Thus can the poet get the modern curse,
Coronary thrombosis, into verse.
"Modern," I say. This fashionable bane
Is not described by Shakespeare—or by Jane.
It's not a thing those knights in armour had,
Nor is it mentioned in the Iliad.
It is, as many other evils are,
Almost coeval with the motor-car.
But now, they say, it is the reason why
One-fifth of those who die in Britain die.
There are two schools of thought. One tells you flat
It comes of taking too much animal fat.
This breeds Cholesterol: and so they damn
Such lights of life as butter, milk, and ham.
The other school insists, with my applause,
That these nutritious foods are *not* the cause.
They know of Africans who eat and drink
Fats all the time—but always in the pink:
And when they die, which is extremely rare,
You'll find that no Cholesterol is there.
The reason is, these enviable men
Take healthy exercise from 10 till 10.
But we, the best and brightest in the town,
Spend nearly all the daylight sitting down.
Not Sloth, not Indolence, have damped our fires
But the soft slogging that Success requires.
We sit to work in motor, bus, or train,
Sit at our work, and, homing, sit again:
The "active" man, forever in a fuss,
Must do more sitting than the rest of us.
The more he telephones the more he sits,
Yet exercises nothing but his wits.
At golf they use the little legs, no doubt,
But other men must cart the clubs about.
Tycoon or Clerk, accept the same prognosis—
You're heading for *coronary thrombosis.*
Be your own caddy; be afraid of chairs;
Ignore that lift and saunter up the stairs.

Do not be jet whizz over to Quebec;
But go by ship and march about the deck.
    And no retiring to "a life of ease"—
For here's the certainty of heart disease.
    It will be best not only for your soul
To weed the garden and bring in the coal.
    And pray each evening for a transport strike—
Thus you may live as long as you would like.

—A.P.H.

*"Good Heavens, Lavinia! It says here the East Wing was
burned down last night."*

HIGH, WIDE AND HANDSOME

BASIL BOOTHROYD in praise of jetting

A LONDON clubman in one of Anthony Powell's early books feels obliged to excuse the cut of his dress suit: "I bought it in Athens before the war." This was the first war, of course. But I was reading it before the second, and the line stuck in my head as a sizzlingly sophisticated throwaway. Not the dress suit. Never mind that. I'd got one of those myself around that time, for the Farmers' Ball, Horncastle, Lincs, and any excuse I may have offered for its cut would just have been about misunderstandings over the postal measurement form. Well, I suppose I might have said that I'd had it made in London, which would have been impressive enough in terms of romantic places . . . But Athens! It was as remote from visitable reality as Ursa Major. (I was going to say the moon: you have to keep updating your idiom these days.)

Well. By the time you read this I shall have been in Athens last Wednesday, if that isn't too confusing. Three and a half hours from London's umbrellas, and the sun comes whanging off the Parthenon and associated buildings like a flaming arrow. From the babel of Heathrow's loudspeakers to the sprawling buzz of the basking drinkers in Syntagma Square . . . and trying to believe, for one's conscience's sake, that those damned Colonels are really throwing their shadow over it all.

What? Well, yes, there's the money. But I don't suppose the dress-suit man went for nothing. It was also less convenient. Let's see now—a hansom from the club to Victoria, unload bags, count them on to the Dover train, fight for porters, choppy old crossing to Calais, fight again; Paris, change trains, hang around; Basle, I suppose: Trieste, Zagreb or somewhere—I don't know, I've never done it, and never shall now—Sarajevo, a dump without even a niche in history at this time, and sounds just the place to lose the luggage and find you're on a stopping train to Sofia by mistake. An anxious business, and long. Poor upholstery, no free meals, no hostesses in cute hats, or confident messages handed back from the chef du train saying you're just passing over the Jungfrau and you've only an hour or so to go. Your pre-1914 dress suit man, if he only had a fortnight's leave to do his romantic foreign shopping, would have to be in and out of his Kolokotroni Street tailor's pretty smartly if he didn't want to miss the train back. Coat? No idea. But I'll bet his hairdresser couldn't manage it. My hairdresser's jetting to Venice this year, and my wife's, for reasons best known, to Budapest. Oh, yes, since the Wright Brothers first got off the ground, through a long line of improvements right up to Frank Whittle, you can be seven days away from the office and still spend six and a half of them in Malaga, trying to forget the boss. The only risk is that he may be there too—though possibly not under the terms of your cut-price package deal, which seems to work out, by some inscrutable mystery of accountancy, about the same as a quick burst round the Lake District.

Who wants speed? The question is put. I've put it before now. How can rushing about the sky at six hundred miles an hour, they say, compare with the murmurous rhythm of the train wheels, the exciting glimpses of Dijon station at midnight, with actual French railwaymen rolling genuine French milk-churns? It's a matter of opinion, naturally. What most appeals to you about Rimini, Estoril, Corfu—being there or getting there? Only an idiot, surely, would say . . . But you've a right to your opinion. Mine is that if you're so long getting to Naples that you haven't time for a sniff round Pompeii you might as well save your money and wait for a good travelogue to hit your local Odeon.

An unnaturally rapid change of scene, they say, is upsetting to the system. Unnatural, too. Perhaps so, for people who've lost their childhood appetite for spells. The magic carpet and the seven-league boots seemed so delicious; it was part of life's great disillusionment to grow up and find they never lifted off the pages of the book. But here they are, and it's the unnaturalness that's half the fun. Don't tell me the stagnant spirit isn't refreshed by a neat trick like breakfast in Belsize Park and tea in Toronto (not that I've ever had either, but you must get your alliteration where you can). Even on the smallest scale I respond: even to the bit of piston-engine wand-waving that hops me in twenty minutes from Lydd to Le Touquet—suddenly, in the time it takes to write a postcard saying you're off all right, here are all these new people, wearing berets and yesterday's shave and talking in a strange tongue. Beat that, Merlin.

Although it's passed through a lot of comics and disc-jockeys since then, that was originally a *Punch* joke about the caterpillar saying to the butterfly, "You'll never get me up in one of those things." Poor, deluded caterpillar, thinking it could avoid the inevitable. We all fly eventually. The interviewed centenarian can't stagger the readers any more with that old gag about never having been in a train or seen the sea. It's never having flown or seen the Mediterranean (at the least) that astounds us these days. My wife came the caterpillar line for years. I blamed in on the wealth of old telefilms that keep trying to wring another squawk out of the plot that has the pilot and co-pilot unconscious from an obscure virus, and a hundred passengers being talked down by ground control, with a man at the instrument panel who doesn't know his air-speed indicator from an eight-day alarm clock, not to mention fog closing in down below and a time-bomb hidden in the baggage compartment. (They're still running these films, I notice, mostly in our last fortnight before take-off.) I don't know what it was that got her up there in the end. Possibly a wealth of old telefilms about the *Titanic*, timed to coincide with our riffle through the cruise brochures. But she gave up struggling around at sea-level in the end, unstuck her countless little aching feet, sprouted wings, and began flitting from tarmac to tarmac with the abandonment of a Rod Laver.

But with less frequency, of course, which is the secret of success. If all airports look the same, how much truer of all tennis-courts? Commuting between Wimbledon, Forest Hills, Paris, Mexico City, Buenos Aires, and nothing to choose between them but the umpire's accent—this must certainly wipe a lot of the wizardry off it: though Laver and Co. may not mind missing the magic; they reap a few material advantages. Much as we love them, when they deign to drop out of their giddy circuit on to our own patch from time to time, they'd soon find us losing interest if they didn't scoop up their rackets and prize money and jet off elsewhere for a bit. Theirs is a short earning life. As long as you can manage Los Angeles today and Bournemouth tomorrow you can keep up the optimum take. Uneconomical loitering around by train, boat and bus could make the thing hardly worth going in for.

Airborne statesmen, on the other hand, probably don't feel even this much affection for the ten-miles-a-minute world, and could make out a better anti-Whittle case than anyone. Harold Wilson can whizz from Whitehall to the White House without bettering his £14,000 p.a. by a bob, and must look back wistfully to the restful times of Gladstone and Disraeli. If they ever went anywhere, and I don't know that they did, they had six or seven quiet weeks in transit to get their notes together. Five hours, and not knowing whether your stomach's lunched twice or not, adds a pressure to life that you didn't bargain for when you climbed the Huyton hustings twenty years back.

Still, never mind the tennis players and politicians. Don't even worry about the high-speed boredom of David Frost. They're overdoing it, and it's not the jet turbine's fault. For you and me, twice a year maximum into the wild blue yonder, it's great. Beats your stage-coach and mule any time. Agreed?

See you in Venice, perhaps . . . Algiers, Garda, Taormina, Nairobi . . . Even Athens. But you'll have to hurry to catch me there. That was last week.

Mr. William Clark, solicitor, said Martin had indulged himself very considerably and could not remember doing what he was charged with. He had promised his family that he would not touch whisky again and had taken up the hobby of breeding canaries, which he hoped would cool him down a bit.

(Stirling Observer)

Entertaining the
Very Special Guest

B. A. YOUNG

WE all know, do we not, those occasions when our guests—without realising it, bless them!—set us problems that somehow do not seem amenable to solution by any of the ordinary rules. From the pages of my guest-book I have selected four meals this week that have been devised to meet just this kind of difficulty

For a Middle-Eastern Potentate

My first menu is devised for that tricky evening when you have to entertain an influential sheikh from some rich oil-kingdom in the Middle East. Sheikhs are famous for their hospitality, and I am sure we have all spent happy evenings in some Arabian tent, remembering always, as we are handed the choicest morsels, to eat them with our right hands lest we offer an unintended insult to our host. What more suitable, then, than to tender the visiting sheikh hospitality after his own fashion?

For a simple but appropriate menu I suggest:

Couscous aux Yeux d'Agneaux
Rahat Lakoum
Sherbet

For the *couscous*, prepare a basic mutton stew and simmer for eight hours over a moderate bonfire in a heavy iron pot. While it is cooking, seethe the eyeballs of two young lambs and boil for half an hour in white wine (or cider will do). Add these to the *couscous* just before you serve it, drawing attention to them every time your guest seems inclined to help himself to some other piece of meat, just as he did for you when he was host and you his guest.

If lamb's eyes are not obtainable, you can get bull's eyes at your local confectioners while you are shopping for your *rahat lakoum* and your sherbet.

Next week, for the benefit of those of you who may be entertaining chieftains from wilder parts of the globe, I will give my special recipe for Mock Man.

My next meal is

For a Rock 'n' Roll Singer

Do not make the mistake of underestimating the knowledge of "good living" which these boys acquire on their rapid ascent from the assembly-line to the Golden Disc. They will soon scent condescension if you invite them for a special celebration and offer them nothing more than steak, chips and peas.

On the other hand, do not go so far in the other direction that they become involved in knife-and-fork trouble, which may ruin a whole evening for them. My suggestion for an unusual but acceptable meal to offer to Master Teddy Jeans when you celebrate the dissolution of his contract with his latest manager is as follows:

Sweet Corn
Bouquet de Crevettes Roses
Asparagus
Petit fours

Serve the sweet corn on individual soup-plates, with little stakes in each end to hold it by, and small individual sauce-boats of *beurre fondu* to pour over it. The *crevettes* should be broken open before serving, or at any rate marked with dotted lines, to show which bits must be detached—though no one with experience of coping with shrimps should go astray with these, their big brothers.

More butter goes with the asparagus. The beauty of this somewhat unorthodox menu is that all the items in it are by custom eaten with the fingers, and so no knives and forks are needed at all. All that is required is a finger-bowl, and perhaps a comb if your guest makes heavy weather with the asparagus.

Third on my list is a rather special meal

For a Wealthy Relation

We have all at some time faced the problem of getting rid of a rich relative from whom we have expectations, by means of some tasteless but effective item served at an appropriate moment during the meal; but there is always the difficulty of deciding just what is the right time to serve it and the most elegant method of administration.

For a meal that would not disgrace a Borgia, here is a suitable menu:

Ravioli al Sugo
Chicken Vol-au-Vent
Croquettes de Riz
Bombe Surprise

What is so peculiarly "right" about this menu is that every item comes to the table as it were "parcelled up" in little containers, into *any one of which* the critical ingredient may be introduced. This will enable your guest to enjoy the whole meal in a contentment and relaxation suited to the excellence of your *cuisine*.

The meal should be followed by strong black coffee—a good quality *arabica* is better than a *robusta*—and a liqueur. The coup should of course be given with the liqueur. This enables the whole of the meal to be eaten and avoids the risk of broken glass and crockery inseparable from a sudden collapse at the dining-table.

Now here is a rather special meal which I have devised

For an Empire Loyalist

Empire Loyalists are often hard to entertain, as they shy away from such dishes as borstch, caviar, pirozhki, and so on, and must usually be contented with some conventional but characteristically Commonwealth food such as roast Canterbury lamb from New Zealand or a Welsh Rabbit of Canadian Cheddar. I only learnt how to achieve the truly individual touch I was looking for when I discovered the one garnish indispensable in every loyal kitchen—methylene blue.

With methylene blue, a tasteless blue colouring, a suitable menu can be prepared in an endless variety of ways. For this week I am going to suggest:

Tartelette Union Jack
Suprême de Volaille Lady Houston
Cabinet Pudding
Petit Gervais aux Fraises et Methylene Blue

For your tart, line a square dish with short pastry and fill with a thick *béchamel* sauce. While it is setting, prepare a paste from ½ oz. butter and the same quantity of flour, adding methylene blue drop by drop until it is a deep ultramarine. Roll this out very thin, and with it and some strips of red pimento decorate your tart in the pattern of the Union Jack and bake in a moderate oven.

For the *suprême de volaille,* choose only the whitest meat from the breast of the chicken, and serve it flanked on one side by baked tomatoes and on the other by mashed potatoes coloured with a little methylene blue.

You will not need any methylene blue for my way of doing Cabinet Pudding. Simply prepare it according to the usual recipe and then toss sufficient raw eggs and soft fruit against it to satisfy the appetite of any Empire Loyalist confronted with something labelled "Cabinet".

Finally, I would like to suggest a light informal supper

For Mr. Norman Collins

Or, indeed, for anyone else concerned with the independent television industry, where money flows like Chateau Yquem. I am going to offer them:

Pâté of Nightingales' Tongues
Caviar aux Blinis
Ortolans aux Truffes
Roast Sucking Pig
Peaches in Champagne

First catch your nightingales . . . but no. Mr. Collins has but to clap his hands and nightingales will come flocking to him, hoping for contracts.

A Word About Dinners
William Makepeace Thackeray

NGLISH Society, my beloved Bob, has this eminent advantage over all other—that is, if there be any society left in the wretched distracted old European continent—that it is above all others a dinner-giving society. A people like the Germans, that dines habitually, and with what vast appetite I need not say, at one o'clock in the afternoon—like the Italians, that spends its evenings in Opera boxes—like the French, that amuses itself of nights with *eau sucrée* and intrigue —cannot, believe me, understand Society rightly. I love and admire my nation for its good sense, its manliness, its friendliness, its morality in the main—and these, I take it, are all expressed in that noble institution, the dinner.

The dinner is the happy end of the Briton's day. We work harder than the other nations of the earth. We do more, we live more in our time, than Frenchmen or Germans. Every great man amongst us likes his dinner, and takes to it kindly. I could mention the most august names of poets, statesmen, philosophers, historians, judges, and divines, who are great at the dinner-table as in the field, the closet, the senate, or the bench. Gibbon mentions that he wrote the first two volumes of his history whilst a placeman in London, lodging in St. James's, going to the House of Commons, to the Club, and to dinner every day. The man flourishes under that generous and robust regimen; the healthy energies of society are kept up by it; our friendly intercourse is maintained; our intellect ripens with the good cheer, and throws off surprising crops, like the fields about Edinburgh, under the influence of that admirable liquid, claret. The best wines are sent to this country therefore; for no other deserves them as ours does.

I am a diner-out, and live in London. I protest, as I look back at the men and dinners I have seen in the last week, my mind is filled with manly respect and pleasure. How good they have been! how admirable the entertainments! how worthy the men!

Let me, without divulging names, and with a cordial gratitude, mention a few of those whom I have met and who have all done their duty.

Sir, I have sat at table with a great, a world-renowned

statesman. I watched him during the progress of the banquet—I am at liberty to say that he enjoyed it like a man.

On another day, it was a celebrated literary character. It was beautiful to see him at his dinner: cordial and generous, jovial and kindly, the great author enjoyed himself as the great statesman—may he long give us good books and good dinners!

Yet another day, and I sat opposite to a Right Reverend Bishop. My lord, I was pleased to see good thing after good thing disappear before you; and think no man ever better became that rounded episcopal apron. How amiable he was! how kind! He put water into his wine. Let us respect the moderation of the Church.

And then the men learned in the law: how they dine! what hospitality, what splendour, what comfort, what wine! As we walked away very gently in the moonlight, only three days since, from the ————s', a friend of my youth and myself, we could hardly speak for gratitude: "Dear sir,"—we breathed fervently, "ask us soon again." One never has too much at those perfect banquets—no hideous headaches ensue, or horrid resolutions about adopting Revalenta Arabica for the future—but contentment with all the world, light slumbering, joyful waking to grapple with the morrow's work. Ah, dear Bob, those lawyers have great merits! There is a dear old judge at whose family table, if I could see you seated, my desire in life would be pretty nearly fulfilled. If you make yourself agreeable there, you will be in a fair way to get on in the world. But you are a youth still. Youths go to balls: men go to dinners.

Doctors, again, notoriously eat well; when my excellent friend Sangrado takes a bumper, and saying, with a shrug and a twinkle of his eye, *"Video meliora proboque, deteriora sequor,"* tosses off the wine, I always ask the butler for a glass of that bottle.

The inferior clergy, likewise, dine very much and well. I don't know when I have been better entertained, as far as creature comforts go, than by men of very Low Church principles; and one of the very best repasts that ever I saw in my life was at Darlington, given by a Quaker.

Some of the best wine in London is given to his friends by a poet of my acquaintance. All artists are notoriously fond of dinners, and invite you, but not so profusely. Newspaper editors delight in dinners on Saturdays, and give them, thanks to the present position of Literature, very often and good. Dear Bob, I have seen the mahoganies of many men.

Every evening between 7 and 8 o'clock, I like to look at the men dressed for dinner, perambulating the western districts of our city. I like to see the smile on their countenances lighted up with an indescribable self-importance and good humour; the askance glances which they cast at the little street-boys and foot-passengers who eye their shiny boots; the dainty manner in which they trip over the pavement on those boots, eschewing the mud-pools and dirty crossings; the refreshing whiteness of their linen; the coaxing twiddle which they give to the ties of their white chokers—the caress of a fond parent to an innocent child.

I like walking myself. Those who go in cabs or broughams, I have remarked, have not the same radiant expression which the pedestrian exhibits. A man in his own brougham has anxieties about the stepping of his horse, or the squaring of the groom's elbows, or a doubt whether Jones's turn-out is not better; or whether something is not wrong in the springs; or whether he shall have the brougham out if the night is rainy. They always look tragical behind the glasses. A cab diner-out has commonly some cares, lest his sense of justice should be injured by the overcharge of the driver (these fellows are not uncommonly exorbitant in their demands upon gentlemen whom they set down at good houses); lest the smell of tobacco left by the last occupants of the vehicle (five medical students, let us say, who have chartered the vehicle, and smoked cheroots from the London University to the playhouse in the Haymarket) should infest the clothes of Tom Lavender who is going to Lady Rosemary's; lest straws should stick unobserved to the glutinous lustre of his boots—his shiny ones, and he should appear in Dives's drawing-room like a poet with a *tenui avena*, or like Mad Tom in the play. I hope, my dear Bob, if a straw should ever enter a drawing-room in the wake of your boot, you will not be much disturbed in mind. Hark ye, in confidence: I have seen ———[1] in a hack-cab. There is no harm in employing one. There is no harm in anything natural, any more.

I cannot help here parenthetically relating a story which occurred in my own youth, in the year 1815, at the time when I first made my own entrée into society (for everything must have a beginning, Bob; and though we have been gentlemen long before the Conqueror, and have always consorted with gentlemen, yet we had not always attained that *haute volée* of fashion which has distinguished some of us subsequently); I recollect, I say, in 1815, when the Marquis of Sweetbread was good enough to ask me and the late Mr. Ruffles to dinner, to meet Prince Schwartzenberg and the Hetman Platoff. Ruffles was a man a good deal about town in those days, and certainly in very good society.

I was myself a young one, and thought Ruffles was rather inclined to patronize me: which I did not like. "I would have you to know, Mr. Ruffles," thought I, "that, after all, a gentleman can but be a gentleman; that though we Browns have no handles to our names, we are quite as well-bred as some folks who possess those ornaments"—and in fine I determined to give him a lesson. So when he called for me in the hackney-coach at my lodgings in Swallow Street, and we had driven under the porte-cochère of Sweetbread House, where two tall and powdered domestics in the uniform of the Sweetbreads, viz. a spinach-coloured coat, with waistcoat and

[1]Mr. Brown's MS. here contains a name of such prodigious dignity out of the P—r-ge, that we really do not dare to print it.

the rest of delicate yellow or melted-butter colour, opened the doors of the hall—what do you think, sir, I did? In the presence of these gentlemen, who were holding on at the door, I offered to toss up with Ruffles heads or tails, who should pay for the coach; and then purposely had a dispute with the poor Jarvey about the fare. Ruffles's face of agony during this transaction I shall never forget. Sir, it was like the Laocoon. Drops of perspiration trembled on his pallid brow, and he flung towards me looks of imploring terror that would have melted an ogre. A better fellow than Ruffles never lived—he is dead long since, and I don't mind owning to this harmless little deceit.

A person of some note—a favourite Snob of mine—I am told, when he goes to dinner, adopts what he considers a happy artifice, and sends his cab away at the corner of the street; so that the gentleman in livery may not behold its number, or that the lord with whom he dines, and about whom he is always talking, may not be supposed to know that Mr. Smith came in a hack-cab.

A man who is troubled with a shame like this, Bob, is unworthy of any dinner at all. Such a man must needs be a sneak and a humbug, anxious about the effect which he is to produce: uneasy in his mind: a donkey in a lion's skin: a small pretender—distracted by doubts and frantic terrors of what is to come next. Such a man can be no more at ease in his chair at dinner than a man is in the fauteuil at the dentist's (unless indeed he go to the admirable Mr. Gilbert in Suffolk Street, who is dragged into this essay for the benfit of mankind alone, and who, I vow, removes a grinder with so little pain, that all the world should be made aware of him)—a fellow, I say, ashamed of the original from which he sprang, of the cab in which he drives, awkward, therefore, affected, and unnatural, can never hope or deserve to succeed in society.

The great comfort of the society of great folks is, that they do not trouble themselves about your twopenny little person, as smaller persons do, but take you for what you are—a man kindly and good-natured, or witty and sarcastic, or learned and eloquent, or a good raconteur, or a very handsome man (and in '15 some of the Browns were—but I am speaking of five-and-thirty years ago), or an excellent gourmand and judge of wines—or what not. Nobody sets you so quickly at your ease as a fine gentleman. I have seen more noise made about a knight's lady than about the Duchess of Fitzbattleaxe herself: and Lady Mountararat, whose family dates from the Deluge, enters and leaves a room, with her daughters, the lovely Ladies Eve and Lilith d'Arc, with much less pretension and in much simpler capotes and what-do-you-call-'ems, than Lady de Mogyns or Mrs Shindy, who quit an assembly in a whirlwind as it were, with trumpets and alarums like a stage king and queen.

But my pen can run no further, for my paper is out, and it is time to dress for dinner. Let us resume this theme next week, dear youth, and believe me in the meantime to be your affectionate   BROWN THE ELDER.

ON SOME OLD CUSTOMS OF THE DINNER-TABLE

OF all the sciences which have made a progress in late years, I think, dear Bob (to return to the subject from which I parted with so much pleasure last week), that the art of dinner-giving has made the most delightful and rapid advances. Sir, I maintain, even now with a matured age and appetite, that the dinners of this present day are better than those we had in our youth, and I can't but be thankful at least once in every day for this decided improvement in our civilisation. Those who remember the usages of five-and-twenty years back will be ready, I am sure, to acknowledge this progress. I was turning over at the Club yesterday a queer little book written at that period, which, I believe, had some authority at the time, and which records some of those customs which obtained, if not in good London Society, at least in some companies, and parts of our island. Sir, many of these practices seem as anti-quated now as the usages described in the accounts of Homeric feasts, or Queen Elizabeth's banquets and breakfasts. Let us be happy to think they are gone.

The book in question is called *The Maxims of Sir Morgan O'Doherty*, a queer baronet, who appears to have lived in the first quarter of the century, and whose opinions the antiquarian may examine, not without profit—a strange barbarian indeed it is, and one wonders that such customs should ever have been prevalent in our country.

Fancy such opinions as these having ever been holden by any set of men among us. Maxim 2: "It is laid down in fashionable life that you must drink champagne after white cheeses, water after red." . . . "Ale is to be avoided, in case a wet night is to be expected, as should cheese also." Maxim 4: "A fine singer, after dinner, is to be avoided, for he is a great bore, and stops the wine . . . One of the best rules (to put him down) is to applaud him most vociferously as soon as he has sung the first verse, as if all was over, and say to the gentleman farthest from you at table that you admire the conclusion of this song very much." Maxim 25: "You meet people occasionally who tell you it is bad taste to give champagne at dinner—port and Teneriffe being such superior drinking," &c., &c. I am copying out of a book printed three months since describing ways prevalent when you were born. Can it be possible, I say, that England was ever in such a state?

Was it ever a maxim in "fashionable life" that you were to drink champagne after white cheeses? What was that [maxim in] fashionable life about drinking and about cheese? The maxim in fashionable life is to drink what you will. It is too simple now to trouble itself about wine or about cheese. Ale again is to be avoided, this strange Doherty says, if you expect a wet night—and in another place says, "the English drink a pint of porter at a draught."—What English? gracious powers! Are we a nation of coalheavers? Do we ever have a wet night? Do we ever meet people occasionally who say that to give champagne at dinner is bad taste, and that port and Teneriffe are such superior drinking? Fancy Teneriffe, my dear boy—I say fancy a man asking you to drink Teneriffe at dinner; the mind shudders at it—he might as well invite you to swallow the Peak.

And then consider the maxim about the fine singer who is to be avoided. What! was there a time in most people's memory when folks at dessert began to sing? I have heard such a thing at a tenants' dinner in the country; but the idea of a fellow beginning to perform a song at a dinner-party in London fills my mind with terror and amazement; and I picture to myself any table which I frequent, in Mayfair, in Bloomsbury, in Belgravia, or where you will, and the pain which would seize upon the host and the company if some wretch were to commence a song.

We have passed that savage period of life. We do not want to hear songs from guests, we have the songs done for us: as we don't want our ladies to go down into the kitchen and cook the dinner any more. The cook can do it better and cheaper. We do not desire feats of musical or culinary skill—but simple, quiet, easy, unpretending conversation.

In like manner, there was a practice once usual, and which still lingers here and there, of making complimentary speeches after dinner; that custom is happily almost entirely discontinued. Gentlemen do not meet to compliment each other profusely, or to make fine phrases. Simplicity gains upon us daily. Let us be thankful that the florid style is disappearing.

I once shared a bottle of sherry with a commercial traveller at Margate who gave a toast or a sentiment as he filled every glass. He would not take his wine without this queer ceremony before it. I recollect one of his sentiments, which was as follows: "Year is to 'er that doubles our joys, and divides our sorrows—I give you woman, sir,"—and we both emptied our glasses. These lumbering ceremonials are passing out of our manners, and were found only to obstruct our free intercourse. People can like each other just as much without orations, and be just as merry without being forced to drink against their will.

And yet there are certain customs to which one clings still; for instance, the practice of drinking wine with your neighbour, though wisely not so frequently indulged in as of old, yet still obtains and I trust will never be abolished. For though, in the old time, when Mr. and Mrs. Fogy had sixteen friends to dinner, it became an unsupportable *corvée* for Mr. F. to ask sixteen persons to drink wine, and a painful task for Mrs. Fogy to be called upon to bow to ten gentlemen, who desired to have the honour to drink her health, yet, employed in moderation, that ancient custom of challenging your friends to drink is a kindly and hearty old usage, and productive of many most beneficial results.

I have known a man of a modest and reserved turn (just like your old uncle, dear Bob, as no doubt you were going to remark), when asked to drink by the host, suddenly lighten up, toss off his glass, get confidence, and begin to talk right and left. He wanted but the spur to set him going. It is supplied by the butler at the back of his chair.

It sometimes happens, again, that a host's conversational powers are not brilliant. I own that I could point out a few such whom I have the honour to name among my friends—gentlemen, in fact, who wisely hold their tongues because they have nothing to say which is worth the hearing or the telling, and properly confine themselves to the carving of the mutton and the ordering of the wines. Such men, manifestly, should always be allowed, nay encouraged, to ask their guests to take wine. In putting that question, they show their goodwill, and cannot possibly betray their mental deficiency. For example, let us suppose Jones, who has been perfectly silent all dinner-time, oppressed, doubtless, by that awful Lady Tiara, who sits swelling on his right hand, suddenly rallies, singles me out, and with a loud cheering voice, cries, "Brown, my boy, a glass of wine." I reply, "With pleasure, my dear Jones." He responds as quick as thought, "Shall it be hock or champagne, Brown?" I mention the wine which I prefer. He calls to the butler, and says, "Some champagne or hock" (as the case may be, for I don't choose to commit myself),—"some champagne or hock to Mr. Brown"; and finally he says, "Good health!" in a pleasant tone. Thus, you see, Jones, though not a conversationist, has had the opportunity of making no less than four observations, which, if not brilliant or witty, are yet manly, sensible, and agreeable. And I defy any man in the metropolis, be he the most accomplished, the most learned, the wisest, or the most eloquent, to say more than Jones upon a similar occasion.

If you have had a difference with a man, and are desirous to make it up, how pleasant it is to take wine with him! Nothing is said but that simple phrase which has just been uttered by my friend Jones; and yet it means a great deal. The cup is a symbol of reconciliation. The other party drinks up your goodwill as you accept his token of returning friendship—and thus the liquor is hallowed which Jones has paid for: and I like to think that the grape which grew by Rhine or Rhone was born and ripened under the sun there, so as to be the means of bringing two good fellows together. I once heard the head physician of a hydropathic establishment on the sunny banks of the first-named river, give the health of His Majesty the King of Prussia, and, calling upon the company to receive that august toast with a "donnerndes Lebehoch," toss off a bumper of sparkling water. It did not seem to me a genuine enthusiasm. No, no, let us have toast and wine, not toast and water. It was not in vain that grapes grew on the hills of Father Rhine.

One seldom asks ladies now to take wine,—except when, in a confidential whisper to the charming creature whom you have brought down to dinner, you humbly ask permission to pledge her, and she delicately touches her glass with a fascinating smile, in reply to your glance,—a smile, you rogue, which goes to your heart. I say, one does not ask ladies any more to take wine: and I think, this custom being abolished, the contrary practice should be introduced, and that the ladies should ask the gentlemen. I know one who did, *une grande dame de par le monde*, as honest Brantôme phrases it, and from whom I deserved no such kindness—but, sir, the effect of that graceful act of hospitality was such, that she made a grateful slave for ever of one who was an admiring rebel previously, who would do anything to show his gratitude, and who now knows no greater delight that when he receives a card which bears her respected name.[1]

A dinner of men is well now and again, but few well-regulated minds relish a dinner without women. There are some wretches who, I believe, still meet together for the sake of what is called "the spread," who dine each other round and round, and have horrid delights in turtle, early peas, and other culinary luxuries—but I pity the condition as I avoid the banquets of those men. The only substitute for ladies at dinners, or consolation for want of them, is—smoking. Cigars, introduced with the coffee, do, if anything can, make us forget the absence of the other sex. But what a substitute is that for her who doubles our joys, and divides our griefs! for woman!—as my friend the traveller said.   BROWN THE ELDER.

[1]Upon my word, Mr. Brown, this is too broad a hint.—*Punch*.

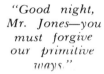

"Good night, Mr. Jones—you must forgive our primitive ways."

GREAT AND LITTLE DINNERS

It has been said, dear Bob, that I have seen the mahoganies of many men, and it is with no small feeling of pride and gratitude that I am enabled to declare also that I hardly remember in my life to have had a bad dinner. Would to Heaven that all mortal men could say likewise! Indeed, and in the presence of so much want and misery as pass under our ken daily, it is with a feeling of something like shame and humiliation that I make the avowal; but I have robbed no man of his meal that I know of, and am here speaking of very humble as well as very grand banquets, the which I maintain are, when there is a sufficiency, almost always good.

Yes, all dinners are good, from a shilling upwards. The plate of boiled beef which Mary, the neat-handed waitress, brings or used to bring you in the Old Bailey—I say used, for, ah me! I speak of years long past, when the cheeks of Mary were as blooming as the carrots which she brought up with the beef, and she may be a grandmother by this time, or a pallid ghost, far out of the regions of beef;—from the shilling dinner of beef and carrots to the grandest banquet of the season—everything is good. There are no degrees in eating. I mean that mutton is as good as venison—beefsteak, if you are hungry, as good as turtle—bottled ale, if you like it, to the full as good as champagne;—there is no delicacy in the world which Monsieur Francatelli or Monsieur Soyer can produce, which I believe to be better than toasted cheese. I have seen a dozen of epicures at a grand table forsake every French and Italian delicacy for boiled leg of pork and peas pudding. You can but be hungry, and eat and be happy.

What is the moral I would deduce from this truth, if truth it be? I would have a great deal more hospitality practised than is common among us—more hospitality and less show. Properly considered, the quality of dinner is twice blest: it blesses him that gives, and him that takes: a dinner with friendliness is the best of all friendly meetings—a pompous entertainment, where no love is, the least satisfactory.

Why, then, do we of the middle classes persist in giving entertainments so costly, and beyond our means? This will be read by many mortals who are aware that they live on leg of mutton themselves, or worse than this, have what are called meat teas, than which I cannot conceive a more odious custom; that ordinarily they are very sober in their way of life; that they like in reality that leg of mutton better than the condiments of that doubtful French artist who comes from the pastrycook's, and presides over the mysterious stewpans in the kitchen; why, then, on their company dinners should they flare up in the magnificent manner in which they universally do?

Everybody has the same dinner in London, and the same soup, saddle of mutton, boiled fowls and tongue, entrées, champagne, and so forth. I own myself to being no better nor worse than my neighbours in this respect, and rush off to the confectioner's for sweets, &c.; hire sham butlers and attendants; have a fellow going round the table with still and dry champagne, as if I knew his name, and it was my custom to drink those wines every day of my life. I am as bad as my neighbours, but why are we so bad, I ask?—why are we not more reasonable?

If we receive very great men or ladies at our houses, I will lay a wager that they will select mutton and gooseberry tart for their dinner; forsaking the entrées which the men in white Berlin gloves are handing round in the Birmingham plated dishes. Asking lords and ladies, who have great establishments of their own, to French dinners and delicacies, is like inviting a grocer to a meal of figs, or a pastrycook to a banquet of raspberry tarts. They have had enough of them. And great folks, if they like you, take no count of your feasts, and grand preparations, and can but eat mutton like men.

One cannot have sumptuary laws nowadays, or restrict the gastronomical more than any other trade: but I wish a check could be put upon our dinner-extravagances by some means, and am confident that the pleasures of life would greatly be increased by moderation. A man might give two dinners for one, according to the present pattern. Half your money is swallowed up in a dessert, which nobody wants in the least, and which I always grudge to see arriving at the end of plenty. Services of culinary kickshaws swallow up money, which gives nobody pleasure, except the pastrycook, whom they enrich. Everybody entertains as if he had three or four thousand a year.

Some one with a voice potential should cry out against this overwhelming luxury. What is mere decency in a very wealthy man is absurdity—nay, wickedness, in a poor one: a frog by nature, I am an insane, silly creature, to attempt to swell myself to the size of the ox, my neighbour. Oh that I could establish in the middle classes of London an Anti-entrée and Anti-dessert movement! I would go down to posterity not ill-deserving of my country in such a case, and might be ranked among the social benefactors. Let us have a meeting at Willis's Rooms, ladies and gentlemen, for the purpose, and get a few philanthropists, philosophers, and bishops or so, to speak! As people, in former days, refused to take sugar, let us get up a society which shall decline to eat dessert and made-dishes.[1]

[1] Mr. Brown here enumerates three entrées, which he confesses he can *not* resist, and likewise preserved cherries at dessert: but the principle is good, though the man is weak.

In this way, I say, every man who now gives a dinner might give two; and take in a host of poor friends and relatives, who are now excluded from his hospitality. For dinners are given mostly in the middle classes by way of revenge; and Mr. and Mrs. Thompson ask Mr. and Mrs. Johnson because the latter have asked them. A man at this rate who gives four dinners of twenty persons in the course of the season, each dinner costing him something very near upon thirty pounds, receives in return, we will say, forty dinners from the friends whom he has himself invited. That is, Mr. and Mrs. Johnson pay a hundred and twenty pounds, as do all their friends, for forty-four dinners of which they partake. So that they may calculate that every time they dine with their respective friends, they pay about twenty-eight shillings per *tête*. What a sum this is, dear Johnson, for you and me to spend upon our waistcoats! What does poor Mrs. Johnson care for all these garish splendours, who has had her dinner at two with her dear children in the nursery? Our custom is not hospitality or pleasure, but to be able to cut off a certain number of acquaintance from the dining list.

One of these dinners of twenty, again, is scarcely ever pleasant as far as regards society. You may chance to get near a pleasant neighbour and neighbouress, when your corner of the table is possibly comfortable. But there can be no general conversation. Twenty people cannot engage together in talk. You would want a speaking-trumpet to communicate from your place by the lady of the house (for I wish to give my respected reader the place of honour) to the lady at the opposite corner at the right of the host. If you have a joke or a *mot* to make, you cannot utter it before such a crowd. A joke is nothing which can only get a laugh out of a third part of the company. The most eminent wags of my acquaintance are dumb in these great parties; and your *raconteur* or story-teller, if he is prudent, will invariably hold his tongue. For what can be more odious than to be compelled to tell a story at the top of your voice, to be called on to repeat it for the benefit of a distant person who has only heard a part of the anecdote? There are stories of mine which would fail utterly were they narrated in any but an undertone; others in which I laugh, am overcome by emotion, and so forth—what I call my *intimes* stories. Now it is impossible to do justice to these except in the midst of a general hush, and in a small circle; so that I am commonly silent. And as no anecdote is positively new in a party of twenty, the chances are so much against you that somebody should have heard the story before, in which case you are done.

In these large assemblies, a wit, then, is of no use, and does not have a chance: a *raconteur* does not get a fair hearing, and both of these real ornaments of a dinner table are thus utterly thrown away. I have seen Jack Jolliffe, who can keep a table of eight or ten persons in a roar of laughter for four hours, remain utterly mute in a great entertainment, smothered by the numbers and the dowager on each side of him: and Tom Yarnold, the most eminent of conversationists, sit through a dinner as dumb as the footman behind him. They do not care to joke unless there is a sympathizing society, and prefer to be silent rather than throw their good things away.

What I would recommend, then, with all my power, is that dinners should be more simple, more frequent, and should contain fewer persons. Ten is the utmost number that a man of moderate means should ever invite to his table; although in a great house, managed by a great establishment, the case may be different. A man and woman may look as if they were glad to see ten people; but in a great dinner they abdicate their position as host and hostess,—are mere creatures in the hands of the sham butlers, sham footmen, and tall confectioners' emissaries who crowd the room,—and are guests at their own table, where they are helped last, and of which they occupy the top and bottom. I have marked many a lady watching with timid glances the large artificial *major-domo*, who officiates for that night only, and thought to myself, "Ah, my dear madam, how much happier might we all be if there were but half the splendour, half the made-dishes, and half the company assembled."

If any dinner-giving person who reads this shall be induced by my representations to pause in his present career, to cut off some of the luxuries of his table, and, instead of giving one enormous feast to twenty persons, to have three simple dinners for ten, my dear Nephew will not have been addressed in vain. Everybody will be bettered; and while the guests will be better pleased, and more numerous, the host will actually be left with money in his pocket. BROWN THE ELDER.

Hostess: *"Must you leave so soon?"*
Celebrity: *"Yes, I* think *everyone has seen me."*

73

Move Over, Sinatra!

KEITH WATERHOUSE does it his way

I DID not groove overmuch in my youth. Naturally one was a swinger within one's limitations—I distinctly remember my mother urging me to "turn that swing off" whenever there was a big band on the Light Programme—but the opportunities for rave-ups were few. The Rex Ballroom lacked the ambience of an Annabelle's or Tramp's; the Squadronaires were not quite the gas that, for example, the Grateful Dead were later to become.

I did not groove to any marked extent in my early manhood either, unless you want to count a couple of suppers in one of those restaurants where they'll let you past the door in a turtle-neck sweater. A man once asked for my autograph in the Establishment Club, but he thought I was Rupert Davies.

Nor have I grooved since. It has always turned out that by the time I discovered where it was all happening, it had all happened. When I tell you that I have only just begun to master The Twist you will have a glimmering of my situation. My clothes are of a style that was vaguely outasight in 1962; my membership cards are for clubs that, if they have not closed down or burned down, have not set eyes on Michael Caine since the reign of Harold Macmillan.

I was just getting to that point in life where you wake up in the wee sma' low-metabolism hours convinced that nature intended you to burn the candle only at one end when it occurred to me that of the several ages of grooving there is one that has not yet passed me by. I refer to the age group loosely encompassing your Sinatras, your Dean Martins, your Robert Mitchums, your Trevor Howards, your David Nivens, and similar hell-raisers and members of clans or rat-packs.

The best, it came to me in the kind of psychedelic flash you would normally associate with the lighting effects in a discotheque had you ever set eyes on one bar on telly, is yet to come. I am but in my forty-third year. Your Sinatras are in their fifty-sixth, and you have only a press officer's word for that. All I need is a Pacific-tanned face looking like pigskin luggage that has been jumped up and down on by enraged airline porters, and I have it within me to become the last of the middle-aged swingers, an improvement on my original plan to develop the paunch and take up stamp-collecting. Give me a lightweight suit, a tuxedo for the odd party to meet Suzie Knickerbocker, a clutch of credit cards, a receding hairline, a set of golf-clubs, a million dollars, a drop or two of after-shave and a nicotine-stained voice, and I shall be set fair for grooving out the evening of my life.

And what is so cunning or far-out about this wheeze is that I have a minimum of twelve years in which to make the transition. That should leave plenty of time for any little snags or hang-ups that might arise as a result of arriving at the grooving scene or bag so late.

These should be few. The reassuring thing about the middle-aged swinger is that he is never to be found actually swinging, so the obvious danger of my becoming the Charlie Twirp of the nineteen-eighties is at one stroke obviated. What you must have noticed about the middle-aged swinger is that he has always just swung. He is not in Las Vegas; he has recently left Las Vegas. He is not in the Peppermint Room on the Golden Strip of Miami Beach: he has quarrelled with the management of the Peppermint Room and shaken the gold-dust of Miami Beach off his canvas sneakers for ever. He is not getting smashed out of his mind in Rome, with subsequent appearances in court on charges of offending public morals; that particular incident, he confesses to the showbiz columnists, was largely invented by the showbiz columnists. All he had to drink in Rome was a sugar-free tonic-water (which admittedly somehow got thrown over a policeman); he has not been in a night-club for five years; and he prefers to spend his evenings in the comfort of his own rocking-chair on ranch or farm, watching late-shows in colour. End quote.

In short, apart from the occasional appearance to raise forty million pounds at a charity concert and the odd bit of jetting in or jetting out to keep the *paparazzi* happy, I can't see why life as a middle-aged swinger should be any more coronary-inducing than the abandoned scheme of becoming a middle-aged stamp collector. Less coronary-inducing, when you think about it, because I will not be risking the excitement of finding a flawed Tristan de Cunha triangular among the jumbo introductory packet. All I need to do is loll in the rocking-chair on ranch or farm or small flat in Marylebone, watching telly and accepting person-to-person calls from Bob Hope, President Nixon or, as they are sometimes called, Earl Mountbatten.

What the middle-aged swinger is up to, of course—and it comes cheaper than playing craps all night long, you must admit—is resting on his laurels. He is the man who has seen it all before, which gives him that cynical appeal so sought-after by twenty-one-year-old blonde birds or chicks. He has drunk the cup of life to the dregs, which explains that slightly pained expression behind the dark glasses, hitherto a puzzling factor when you consider the vast numbers of twenty-one-year-old blonde birds or chicks at his disposal. He has been everywhere and done everything, and this brings us in a roundabout way to snag number one, because I have been nowhere and done nothing. On the other hand, I'm a good liar. Did I ever tell you about that jag on the Golden Strip at Miami Beach? The Peppermint Room? Before that exaggerated bother in Rome? You better believe it.

Looking over the inventory of props, notably the wardrobe of lightweight suits and the million dollars, I see that we may have the makings of snag number two in that I have neither. Call the gear question snag 2(a): this is not insuperable. The polo-neck sweaters that were de rigueur dining-out gear in the Angry Young Man period are still serviceable; add canvas sneakers and pair of old flannels and you have created the casual look, as observed among swingers who have just been playing eighteen holes with Bob or Dino. The million-dollar issue or snag 2(b) is even less insuperable. Middle-aged swingers are supposed to have money but they are never observed actually spending money. This is partly because they have already bought everything that money can buy (including happiness), partly because they never go anywhere, and partly because they have studiously fostered a public reputation for being mean. For *item*, one million dollars, then, read *item*, one crate of sugar-free tonic-water, plus *item*, gratuity to Bob Hope's gag-writers for joke about spider's web in wallet.

What might well crop up as snag number three is that there seems to be some kind of obligation to hit photographers, but I think we can duck that particular fence when we come to it. The only remaining problem is the non-availability of twenty-one-year-old blonde birds or chicks. This could be well-nigh insuperable except for the happy recollection that we have twelve years to think about it.

My plan here is fiendishly simple. The twenty-one-year-old blonde birds or chicks who will accompany me into my swinging middle age are all, at the moment of writing, but mousey-haired schoolgirls. All mousey-haired schoolgirls love hobbies. The thing to do, it seems to me, is start this young people's stamp-collectors' club, later to become the nucleus of a rat-pack. Crazy. Come on in, Francis Albert Sinatra, your time is up.

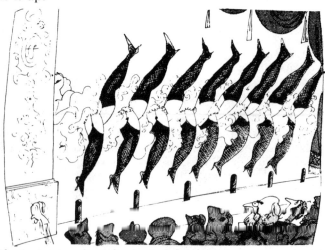

"That's funny, Offenbach, I didn't think I was going to like opera . . ."

PASTA? BASTA!

Paul Dehn

GRAZIE, cameriere! That means "Thank you, waiter!" in Italian, Simon.

No, old chap. Not that way. Look, let Uncle show you. If little Italian boys can eat spaghetti tidily at the age of six, so can little English ones. Now. Hold your fork in your *right* hand and plunge it vertically into the spaghetti, no, Simon, I said *vert—Cameriere! Dell'acqua calda, per favore, subito!* That's Italian for "Some hot water, please, quickly."

Grazie, cameriere.

There. That ought to dry out. You'd better tuck your napkin down your collar and put mine over your trousers. Now, shall we have another go? Plun—I mean put your fork upright into the spaghetti. Good. Now twirl the fork round so that—no, slowly, Simon, *slowly,* not like an egg-whisk. Oh, good grief. *Scusi, Signora. Si. No. No. Si. Cameriere! Dell'acqua calda per la signora alla next* table *e per me un nuevo* napkin.

Grazie, cameriere.

Now don't get discouraged, old chap. Just hang on to your fork. I said hang *on*—oh, Simon. No. Just leave it lying there among the spaghetti. Dammit, Simon, I said *don't* pick it up or you'll get tomato all over your—*CAMERIERE! Un* finger-bowl, *subito.*

Grazie, cameriere.

Now there's nothing to cry about, Simon. It's only a plate of spaghetti and we're going to get it licked, ha, ha, ha.

Better now? Splendid. Just one more go. And please try to listen. Put the fork upright in the spaghetti. Good. Twirl the fork *slowly,* so that you can *collect* the spaghetti *round* it. Very good. Right, you can stop twirling now. Simon, I said STOP twirling, you've collected half a plateful. No, don't *un*twirl or you'll lose the lot, just leave it as it is. Whew.

Now. *Raise* your fork—SLOWLY, Simon—till you've lifted the spaghetti on your *fork* clear of the spaghetti on the *plate.* Go on, lift it. Higher. Higher, Simon. Dammit, if little Italian boys of six can reach, so can little English—all right, stand if you want to. Higher. High—SIMON GET OFF THAT CHAIR OR I'LL BELT THE LIVING—*Cameriere! Ancora dell'acqua calda, per favore, ed un* table-cloth *ed un* bandage *ed un po d'*iodine . . .

Simon, what the hell are you laughing at? Oh. I see. Well, it may interest you to know that "po" is the Italian for "little".

How about packing it in, old chap, and having something simple like—like soup? Certainly not. In a *plate.* No? One last, final bash at the spaghetti? That's the spirit. Here we go then.

Put your fork upright in what's left on the plate. Good. Twirl slowly. Good. Lift it clear. *Very* good. I say, this is exciting, isn't it? Now put the fork in your mouth and don't bother about the bits hanging out—just suck. Suck, Simon. I beg your pardon? Look, I shouldn't bother to try to speak, old chap, it's almost impossible to under—ah. Well, swallow what's actually *in* your mouth and *then* suck.

Suck, Simon. And again. And again. Six inches. Five inches. Four, three, two, one—BRAVO! You've done it, old chap. Congratulations. Your uncle's proud of you. Like it? Mm. Well, it's bound to be a bit cold and greasy, isn't it, after all the time we took. The thing is to eat it quickly while it's still piping hot but that takes a bit of—Simon, are you all right? Have a drink of water, no don't have a drink of water, try putting your head between your legs. No, Simon, between *your* legs. Grab a napkin. No, not *that* napkin—it's full of—*Cameriere! Subitissimo! Un* basin.

An Invitation

*D*EAR *Tom, I hear you're back in Town*
  Bronzed as an Iroquois with brown
    Of sunshine and adventures;
I wish you'd come and dine to-night
Ere stream and hill have faded quite,
And Mammon's dipped you out of sight
    In shares and dull debentures!

You won't get much: my cook of old
You know is not (though gold, pure gold)
    A culinary show thing;
That lady's very utmost word
Is first a sole, and then a bird,
And, if she ventures on a third,
    It's toasted cheese—or nothing!

Forgive my menu its misdeeds,
At least you'll find a Beaune that needs
    No bush's vain adorning,
And when its vinted balms ascend
You'll think, 'Tis thus, though good times end,
Their sunny memories stay to blend
    With fog and Monday morning!

So come. I want to hear about
The Islands,—were the big sea-trout
    As big this year as ever?
And has your brown retriever pup
(Son of old "Shot" who won the Cup)
His father's nose at picking-up?
    He promised to be clever.

You got a stag, I heard from Bee;
The island heads are small, but she
  Says yours is simply ripping;
I want the details of it all,
His points, the ground, the wind, the crawl,
And, flushed with triumph at his fall,
  What sum you spent in tipping!

Our talk shall slip by braes and brooks,
Through several tomes of salmon hooks,
  And on by easy stages
To other works of worthy lore,
Picked from the bookshelf's golden store,
Till round our chairs the very floor
  Is carpeted with sages!

We'll smoke and watch the embers glow
And read the lines we like and know,
  The old, the wise, the witty;
While on the curtained window-pane
You'll hear the patter of the rain,
And down the Knightsbridge Road again
  The roar of London City!

"No, honestly, Mrs. Gibson ...
it's extremely comfortable."

Herbs and Spices

Now that it is becoming increasingly easy to buy herbs in a small shop in Old Compton Street, run personally by Madame Berthe Foulard since 1867, there is no reason why even the least ambitious cook shouldn't have a large country garden full of herbs. Here's a basic selection of the ones you'll be using at every meal.

Estragon Very good with soups, meats, fish, salads, puddings, stews, ice cream, napkins or just boiled and eaten by itself.

Taviot Wonderful with armadillos.

Salkin Milder than taviot, salkin is very good in home-smoked venison. The seeds are quite tasty pickled and chewed, while the leaves, dried and rolled, give a good smoke.

Footle The tall, green, frond-like leaves provide very good camouflage.

Fentury Once widely used in soups, meat, fish and salads, fentury is now chiefly valued for its pungent but not unpleasant taste by the peasants of Haute Dauphiné. Such specialities of the region as Blanquette De Petit Cheval are hardly worth trying if you have no fentury to hand.

Clancy The fluted stalks, if diced and simmered in oil, provide a more than adequate substitute for roast chicken.

Bolster Tied together with salkin, taviot, doggerel, aubrey, fenhoulet, welkin and paragon, bolster makes a very good bouquet garni for stews, soups, meat, fish, salads, gruel and home-made liqueurs.

Cerbic Keeps flies off.

Hallory Only the dried pods are used. They should be hung, dried, ground, pounded, moistened and used very sparingly instead of baked beans on toast. An excellent substitute for dust.

Varnel The classic herb of Tyrolean fish dishes, varnel also makes a very good sort of tea not unlike hot lemonade.

Grass Chopped small, it makes a decorative green garnish on soups, stews, fish, meat, salads and vegetables.

For Beginners

Here is simply all that you will need to do for this tasty suppertime treat: Prepare a "slice" of white bread by cutting it through with a sharp knife to a thickness of approx. ½″ from the end. Your baker will show you how to do this, or may even have in stock a special sort of bread which has already been sliced up by a machine to save you time and worry. Put your completed slice on one side. Next ask your husband to open for you a tin of specially prepared beans in a rich and tasty sauce. Most grocers stock these beans, but in case of difficulty write to me for the name of your nearest stockist. Opening up the delicious aroma is part of the fun of preparing this dish, but it's a man's job and he will probably enjoy helping you about the house. Place the contents into a "saucepan" available from Woolworth's everywhere in a range of pretty colours. Have a packet of butter and a knife to hand and all is now in readiness for you to cook a meal of your own:

Light the gas jet with a match and, *before the match goes out,* also light the grill. This is a valuable economy tip which will help keep down household bills. If you have any difficulty over this first step, ring the number listed under "Electricity Showrooms" and they will be pleased to give you specialist advice. Take a little break now while the grill warms up.

Once you are satisfied that the grill is good and hot (do *not* try and test it with fingers, though!) place your slice of bread in the little pan provided. Soon it will turn a lovely golden brown. This is where the skill and timing comes in. You *must* take out the slice of bread as soon as it is "done to a turn" and then put it back *the other way up.* With practice you will be able to do this very quickly. Now, with the other hand, place the saucepan full of beans on top of the "jet" or "ring" until it makes a funny bubbling noise. Stir. Don't forget to watch for the slice of bread going golden, mouth-watering brown while this is going on. Once it has turned, you take it out, just as before, only this time *you don't put it back.* Put it on a plate instead and get a friend to show you how to butter it. Now comes the tricky bit. As quickly as you can, put all of the bubbly beans on top of the buttered piece of bread (don't spill any!) and then *remember* to turn the jets or rings to the position marked "Off". After several practice goes, you will soon be able to make a pot of tea *at the same time* for a truly magnificent composite feast.

For the Gourmet

Day One: Lightly marinade a handful of Mexican brown beans in a compote of fresh tomatoes, 1 small onion or 2-3 diced shallots, 1 clove of garlic, a sherryglass of marsala, nutmeg, pounded pistachio nuts with the merest hint of basil, ground black pepper and sea-salt to taste. Keep in a cool, dark cellar overnight.

Day Two: First thing in the morning, collect the finest fresh-made yeast and 1 lb.-1½ lb. of wholemeal granary flour with the husks in. Thoroughly steam the oven and bake a classic English loaf (q.v. pages 2-108). Allow to cool and slice deftly with a filleting knife sharpened on carborundum. Introduce the marinade to the light.

Get the grill *thoroughly* hot. There is an old French saying that a chef is made but a *grillardin* is born, so a sliver of fresh bread will require constant attention because half a minute too long means disaster when the heat is so great and an unpleasant charcoaly taste. Bread does not really like being subjected to a blast of dry heat, therefore only first-class produce that will be *al dente* under any circumstances can be cooked in this way. The object is to keep as much moisture and flavour locked in to the spongy centre.

Have prepared the marinade to cook it in a *bain-marie*. The basin will remain at 180°-190°F and that is absolutely right.

This is one of the most *satisfying* ways of cooking.

Using a wooden spatula rinsed in crushed ice, spread the cooled toast liberally with un-salted Provençal butter and, without undue delay, *smother* with the bubbling compote. Garnish with a sprig of borage (Lat. *borago officinalis.* It. *boraggine*) and serve with a fine dry Riesling.

Deep Freeze – Yes or No?

Providing dinner for two, four or even eight guests is comparatively simple. But what if you are expecting fifty or a hundred? This is the position in which many restaurant owners find themselves every night, and at such times they have no hesitation in turning to that most modern of scientific aids—the deep freeze.

"If I'm expecting lots of guests," says Hugh Gentleman, owner/chef of The Last Resort *in the Fulham Road, "the last thing they want me to do is fuss about in the kitchen all evening cooking this and that. It wouldn't be fair on them. I believe passionately in getting all the messy preparations done days, weeks, even years beforehand. Tonight, for instance, I'm giving them a very special Turbot in Maraschino Sauce. What*

would they think if I disappeared after giving them a drink to fiddle around with little cherries for hours, for heaven's sake?

"That's why I spent last Tuesday unpacking the packets from this marvellous little freeze 'n' pack place in Cornwall. Now it's all waiting in the freezer on its plates. At about 6 I'll get them out and warm them up, leaving me plenty of time to dress, mark up wine prices, arrange the flowers and welcome my friends."

But what if some of them decide not to have the Turbot in Maraschino Sauce?

"Now there you've hit upon the perennial headache of the restaurant owner; the guest who decided to ask for something just because it's on the menu. Luckily there's lots of room left in the freezer, so I've stored away the things we didn't use last week. This Blanquette de Veau, for instance—actually, it's Chicken Pilaff now—or this Entrecôte de Something or Other. Do you mind dear? You're sitting on my French dictionary."

*"He loves to potter about in
the lamp."*

Smokers of the World, Unite

P. G. WODEHOUSE

IT can scarcely have escaped the notice of thinking men, I
think, being a thinking man myself, that the forces of
darkness opposed to those of us who like a quiet smoke are
gathering momentum daily and starting to throw their weight
about more than somewhat. Every morning I read in the
papers a long article by another of those doctors who are the
spearhead of the movement. Tobacco, they say, plugs up the
arteries and lowers the temperature of the body extremities,
and if you reply that you like your arteries plugged up and are
all for having the temperature of your body extremities
lowered, especially during the summer months, they bring up
that cat again.

The cat to which I allude is the one that has two drops of
nicotine placed on its tongue and instantly passes beyond the
veil. "Look," they say. "I place two drops of nicotine on the
cat's tongue. Now watch it wilt." I can't see the argument.
Cats, as Charles Stuart Calverley said, may have had their
goose cooked by tobacco juice, but are we to deprive ourselves
of all our modest pleasures just because indulgence in them
would be harmful to some cat which is probably a perfect
stranger?

Take a simple instance such as occurs every Saturday on the
Rugby football field. The ball is heeled out, the scrum half
gathers it, and instantaneously two fourteen-stone forwards
fling themselves on his person, grinding him into the mud.
Must we abolish Twickenham and Murrayfield because some
sorry reasoner insists that if the scrum half had been a cat he
would have been squashed flatter than a Dover sole? And no
use, of course, to try to drive into these morons' heads that
scrum halves are not cats. Really, one feels inclined at times to
give it all up and turn one's face to the wall.

It is pitiful to think that that is how these men spend their
lives, putting drops of nicotine on the tongues of cats day after
day after day. Slaves to a habit, is the way I look at it. But if
you tell them that and urge them to pull themselves together
and throw off the shackles, they just look at you with fishy
eyes and mumble something about it can't be done. Of course
it can be done. All it requires is will power. If they were to say
to themselves "I will not start putting nicotine on cats'
tongues till after lunch" it would be a simple step to knocking
off during the afternoon, and by degrees they would find that
they could abstain altogether. The first cat of the day is the
hard one to give up. Conquer the impulse for the after-
breakfast cat, and the battle is half won.

But how few of them can see this. You think you have
driven home your point, but no. Back comes that fishy-eyed

look, and before you know where you are they are off again with their "Place two drops on the tongue of a cat . . ." The result is that day by day in every way we smokers are being harder pressed. Like the troops of Midian, the enemy prowl and prowl around. First it was James the Second, then Tolstoy, then all these doctors, and now—of all people—Miss Gloria Swanson, who not only has become a non-smoker herself but claims to have converted a San Francisco business man, a Massachusetts dress designer, a lady explorer, a television script writer and a Chicago dentist.

"The joys of not smoking," she says, "are so much greater than the joys of smoking," omitting, however, to mention what the former are. From the fact that she states that her disciples send her flowers, I should imagine that she belongs to the school of thought which holds that abstention from tobacco heightens the sense of smell. "Do you realize," these people tell you, "that if you stop smoking you will be able to smell better?" I don't want to be able to smell better. Living in New York, I often find myself wishing that I didn't smell the place as well as I do.

But I have no quarrel with Miss Swanson. We Wodehouses do not war upon the weaker sex. As far as Miss Swanson is concerned, an indulgent "There, there, foolish little woman" about covers my attitude. The bird I am resolved to expose before the bar of world opinion is the late Count Leo N. Tolstoy.

"Give up smoking? Why?"

For one reason and another I have not read Tolstoy in the original Russian, and it is possible that a faulty translation may have misled me, but what he is recorded as saying in his Essays, Letters and Miscellanies is that an excellent substitute for smoking may be found in twirling the fingers, and there rises before one's mental eye the picture of some big public dinner (decorations will be worn) at the moment when the toast of the Queen is being drunk.

"The Queen!"

"The Queen, God bless her!"

And then.

"Gentlemen, you may twirl your fingers."

It wouldn't work. There would be a sense of something missing. And I don't see that it would be much better if you adopted Tolstoy's other suggestion—viz. playing on the dudka. But then what can you expect of a man who not only wore a long white beard but said that the reason we smoke is to deaden our consciences, instancing the case of a Russian murderer who half-way through the assassination of his employer found himself suffering from cold feet?

"I could not finish the job," he is quoted as saying. "So I went from the bedroom into the drawing-room, sat down there and smoked a cigarette."

"Only when he had stupefied himself with tobacco," says Tolstoy, "did he feel sufficiently fortified to return to the bedroom and finish dispatching the old lady."

Stupefied with tobacco! On a single gasper! They must have been turning out powerful stuff in Russia under the old régime.

And, of course, our own manufacturers are turning out good and powerful stuff today, and what I am leading up to is that we should all avail ourselves of it. Smoke up, my hearties. Never mind Tolstoy. Ignore G. Swanson. Forget the cat. Think what it would mean if for want of our support the tobacco firms had to go out of business. There would be no more of those photographs of authors smoking pipes, and if authors were not photographed smoking pipes, how would we be able to know that they were manly and in the robust tradition of English literature?

A pipe placed on the tongue of an author makes all the difference.

———————

A 25-year-old accounts clerk admitted in court that he had defrauded his employers of more than £233,000 and spent it on high-speed cars, a hotel, a luxury home, land development and a round-the-world trip. He told police when he was arrested: "All my life I've hated being poor." *(Birmingham Mail)*

"Well, gentlemen . . . Shall we join the ladies?"

S. McMURTRY.

Huntin'
MILES KINGTON

I MAY be wrong, but I don't think there has ever been an anti-
blood sports demonstration against angling. We are told it
is the most popular sport in these islands, that up to three
million people go forth regularly hoping to stick a hook
through a fish's eye or mouth, pull it about on the end of a
line for a while and subsequently beat it to death on a stone or
throw it back wounded. And yet no one marches in protest.
Where are the smoke bombs drifting down our salmon streams?
Where are the diversionary tins of worms thrown into the
middle of angling contests? Why does nobody toss thunder-
flashes under the gumboots of the death-dealing fisherman?

Because, I suspect, anglers don't dress up in bright red
fishing costumes and blow horns. They don't mount teams of
horses and gallop through rivers harrying the fish, with
specially trained packs of fish-hounds in full cry before them.
The opposition to fox-hunting is not really based on hatred of
cruelty. (If it were, it would come low down the list of blood
sports, way after coursing, stag-hunting, boxing, football and
motorway driving.) It's based on a dislike of the pageantry
involved in the simple business of getting rid of foxes, the
aristocratic assumptions of the whole thing. The anti-hunting
brigade react to pink coats and the smell of privilege exactly as
fox-hounds react to the scent of a fox. The uninitiated in full
pursuit of the unquotable.

Until Match 7 this year I didn't feel strongly one way or the
other. I grew up in the country, true, but in the hills of Wales
where sport is confined to stealing sheep or hunting for good
restaurants. (Successfully, in the latter case; they have almost
all been eliminated.) So when I was invited out on that damp,
cold, piercing Tuesday morning to follow the Grafton Hunt
in Bedfordshire by car, I arrived with an open mind, three
sweaters and a pleasant open smile which suggested I had no
aerosol tins of aniseed spray about my person.

Keen-eyed readers will have spotted a tell-tale admission
hidden in the undergrowth of that last sentence. By car? How
can you follow the hounds and not be on a horse? For shame!

Those were my feelings also, to begin with. When the
huntsman swept up in his flaming coat with the horn tucked
casually in the front; when the hounds burst ferociously
out of the kennels, poured bloodthirstily towards him and
fawned and wagged round him; when fifteen or twenty riders
assembled on their more or less splendid mounts (and you
forget how big horses are until you find something blocking
out the light and look up at a huge brown thigh muscle) I felt
a hopeless outsider and ready to hate the whole business. Till I
noticed that the hounds were studiously avoiding the horses
and dancing attention on the schoolchildren who had come

out to watch; till I saw that the riders, tight packed in their uniforms, the women's hair netted behind like sausages, were actually chatting to us car-bound mortals, swapping information and prospects.

"Where you heading, Joe?" said John Morris to the huntsman. John was the driver of our car which was actually his car and technical adviser for the whole of this script.

"Up Wakefield way, to draw the woods there," said Joe, a gnarled sixty-two-year-old with a face like crab apples. John nodded approvingly.

"This will be one of the last hunts of the season," he told me confidentially. "Crops are starting to come up and soon most of the fields will be inaccessible. They have to respect the farmers pretty closely—after all, if the farmers cut up rough they could put paid to fox-hunting like a shot. Thirty, forty years ago the hunts didn't give a damn for anybody—most of the farmers were tenants who could be browbeaten—but today it's different. Half the hunt are farmers anyway. See those two girls over there?"

Mmm.

"It's their job to follow at the end of the hunt to close gates, mend broken fences, restore any damage."

"Know where they're heading?" said Frank, a newly arrived friend.

"Up Wakefield way," I said. "Going to draw the woods there." Frank nodded approvingly.

So far I hadn't felt in the least nauseated by hunting. In fact, I found the whole ambiance full of colour and possible excitement. But then, I hadn't yet seen these people leap on a fox and tear it limb from limb. There was plenty of time for nausea yet.

At 11 a.m. the hunt moved off. Colonel This, Mr. That, Major the Other, and Mrs. Everybody trotted away up the lane, and by the time we arrived at the Wakefield woods, there was a line of a dozen cars in the road and twenty-five horses waiting in a track by the trees (because more and more riders kept arriving during the morning) while the hounds were put through the spinney, and the horses then moved off out of sight behind the trees and we could hear the hounds for a bit and then nothing. The possible excitement drained away in minutes of silence.

"How will we know?" I asked John. "When will they? What can we? I mean, is anything going to happen?"

"Have to wait and see," said John. "It's all patience. Could be here half an hour."

We rubbed our hands and peeled our eyes. The wind (by kind permission of Greenland weather effects) drifted through my three sweaters and brought with it sounds of everything except the hounds speaking, which is what they call the frenzied noise of a pack that has smelt a fox. Suddenly the entire hunt reappeared down the track and my blood boiled.

"It was worth it! I got a half pounder."

"That means there's nothing there," said John, and I thought that if a hunt without a fox can look the next best thing to a cavalry charge, a hunt with a fox must look pretty good. The huntsman swept past again, talking to the hounds in a sort of gibberish without consonants. Translated roughly, it meant: "Never mind, let's try the woods on the other side of the road and don't anyone get lost." At least, that's what they did next.

Well, we sat at a corner of the woods and watched the entire hunt go round twice which must have taken half an hour, but the funny thing was that it wasn't boring. There was always the chance that a fox would come sneaking out. Or that the hounds would break into voice. Or that a distant horn would announce their cross-country departure. Or something.

"Look!" said John. "See that animal racing across the field?"

"No!" I said excited.

"Only a hare," he said.

"Where?"

"Gone now." He thought for a moment. "Let's move up the road to that little riding into the wood."

A riding turned out to be a small avenue through the trees. We stared down it. Nothing.

"Look—there's the fox!"

I stared down the riding. Nothing.

"Not in the riding. It came out on the road. It's gone back in."

I stared down the road.

"There it is again. In the riding."

And there it was at last, trotting very sedately across the avenue, low and long, stepping delicately into the trees opposite. And we were the only people who had seen it. The other cars had scattered. The hounds were speaking in the depths of the trees. The horses were miles away. It was a great moment, and shows why following the hunt in a car can be just as creative as following on a horse, if you use your wits and intuition. More, sometimes, since a mobile follower often sees more of the fox and hounds than the horses do.

A minute later the hounds followed the scent across the riding, like a pack of runners after David Bedford. Then the horses came thundering up the road and they all disappeared round the woods. Then nothing.

"I think," said John, "we'll go down the road, turn left and have a look a mile or two beyond."

It's only when you follow a hunt by car that you realise how few roads there are in the country and how many woods, hedges, fields, hills, rises and other things designed for hunts to conceal themselves in. Not a sign of a horse anywhere. I might have given up and gone home. But John kept seeing things and muttering to himself. Wonder why that flock of birds has suddenly taken wing in the woods? . . . those two grazing horses have heard something beyond the hill . . . hello, look at those sheep all bunched up . . . bet the hunt has passed them by . . . And sure enough, we rounded a corner and there suddenly again were the horses, the hounds and the huntsman but not in that order streaming across a field, and I'm here to testify that it's a mighty fine sight especially if you've located it by deduction.

The hunt went on for six hours, raised several foxes and didn't catch any of them that we saw. It didn't matter. The hunt kept getting away from us and we always caught it again, and that was the thrill of the chase for us, if you like. That, and listening to the hunting talk.

"There were some Italian prisoners at Wakefield during the war," said someone during a pause. "They caught a fox one day and cut off its tail, God knows why, then let it go. Now the scent of a fox is all in its brush, you know, so ever after that this fox used to run among the hounds out hunting and they never cottoned on to him."

A likely story. And I've just realised that I forgot to be nauseated by the whole business. Quite the reverse, in fact. All the things they say about hunting are true, but not the whole truth. It is a rich man's sport, but if you turn up with a horse and £3 one day, you can go hunting, and no questions asked. It smells of country privilege, but the one rider I had marked out as a real aristocrat produced the broadest shire accent. And of all the horsey activities—point-to-point, hunt racing, gymkhanas, show jumping—fox-hunting is the only natural, uninhibited, non-artificial one.

I don't think I'll ever take to the horse, and sally forth. But one of these days I'd like to get in a car again and chase after the hunt. I know people say it's cruel to the riders. Secretly, though, I'm convinced they enjoy it.

Notes for Your Party

E. S. TURNER

EVERYONE knows it is wrong to serve guests sturgeon at a round table piled with jasmine, but there is more to entertaining than that.

What better time than Christmas for a fearless examination of our shortcomings as hosts and hostesses? The fault of most of us, as our great-aunts will almost certainly confirm, is that *we just do not take enough trouble.*

Be honest with yourself: when did you last take out the windows of your house in order that the young folks could hold a dance?

Do you simply roll up the carpet and let them get on with it, or do you hire a team of skilled workmen to stretch a glazed dancing cloth over your Aubusson?

You may give your guests cubes of coloured ice to put in their drinks, but do you strew king-size blocks of coloured ice about the house?

So much have our notions of hospitality deteriorated that not everyone will know *why* it is necessary to remove the windows from the frames before holding a dance. It is, as your great-aunt will tell you, only the first step towards ensuring congenial ventilation; the next step is to cover the apertures with artistic draperies of muslin and lace. Also, the external balconies of your house should be enclosed with gay bunting in order to give your guests more sitting-out space. But not wholly enclosed; small windows must be inserted in the coverings, and these in turn must be drapped with lace curtains. Any good do-it-yourself manual will tell you how to build windows in bunting.

The doors of the drawing-room should be removed, too, and replaced by *portière* curtains. It is asking a good deal of a woman to expect her to make an effective entrance through an ordinary doorway.

All this must be done in such a way that sudden gusts of air do not flutter the wax candles (for, surely, you are not depending wholly on electricity?) Even the most worldly-wise escort is sometimes at a loss to know what to do when hot blobs of wax fall on the bare bosom of his lady; and so is the lady. Moreover, the musicians of the Grenadier Guards (hired at 10s. to 15s. per man) cannot always be relied upon to stand fast under this kind of fire; still less can the Yeomanry and Local Volunteers (at 8s. to 10s.).

To decorate your suite you will doubtless have sent out for a supply of exotics from the home garden (or even, at a pinch, from the away garden). But it is important not to overdo things. If your house is well stocked with bronzes, statuary, vases and suits of armour (or even with flights of china geese) you really have no need of floral embellishments. If it is wrong to gild the lily, obviously it is wrong to impose lilies over the gilding.

Only by the observance of points like these can a hostess be sure her dance-floor will not be deserted by midnight, the guests having quietly moved on to another house where the subtleties of hospitality are understood. A hostess nervous of her ground should not shrink from handing over the management of the whole affair, including the guest list, to a lady of higher social status and unquestioned *savoir faire*. The result may well be that her own friends are excluded from her house, but that is a modest price to pay for a reputation as a hostess.

She will be wise to content herself, at first, with entertaining between eighty and two hundred guests; if more than that number are invited the function is, of course, no longer a dance but a ball.

By now the reader may be demanding more specific authority for some of the foregoing statements than the hypothetical word of one or two unidentified great-aunts. The recommendations are those of "A Member of the Aristocracy" who, within the lifetime of some of us, published much-sought-after works with titles like *Manners and Tone of Good Society* and *Society Small Talk*. The full range of his works is hard to chart, but it is unlikely that he was the author of *How She Managed Without a Servant* or *How We Did Without Lodgings at the Seaside*.

Let us, with "A Member of the Aristocracy" at our elbow, consider the giving of dinner parties. The first essential is that whatever food is served should be newly in season. A guest who has been eating salmon at other people's houses when it was 4s. 6d. a pound is not going to thank you if you serve it when the price, as he well knows, has fallen to 1s. 3d. Similarly, if you give him oysters, he has a right to expect that you have paid at least 3s. a dozen for them; and he will wave away plovers' eggs that cost less than 8s. per dozen or spring chickens at less than 9s. 6d. Sweetbreads are fairly safe, because they are always expensive. "Ignorance of when things are in season often causes a hostess to overlook something that has just come in, in favour of something that is just going out." It is true that a willing tradesman is always ready to advise on what is new and expensive, but a hostess ought to know these things for herself.

Not that money should be unnecessarily squandered. A haunch of venison costs £2 2s., but as one can buy half a buck for the same sum, why not?

Although guests appreciate novelty, they will not necessarily be grateful for sturgeon, which is "oftener seen at family dinners than at dinner parties". Eels, for the same reason, should be avoided. Crimped salmon is permissible, even though "kind-hearted women shudder at the idea of thus inflicting deep cuts upon fish that is yet alive" merely in order to make it more digestible.

There may still be a few guests who will not look at saddle of mutton unless it comes from a four-year-old sheep, but their numbers are dwindling. Younger people tend to prefer mutton from two-year-olds.

The custom of serving four *entrées* is also going out. A host's aim should be "to give *entrées* of the highest possible character to tempt the appetite rather than to satisfy it."

Primarily, large dinners are given to please the palates of gentlemen with epicurean tastes. For this reason "it is not expected that ladies should eat of the most highly seasoned and richest dishes given, but should rather select the plainest on the menu". This applies chiefly to young ladies, single or married, for it is recognized that "middle-aged and elderly ladies are at liberty to do pretty well as they please without provoking comment or even observation." In no circumstances, however, should a lady help herself to wine.

In particular, young ladies should decline larks, and especially larks stuffed with oysters (even though there is but one oyster to one lark). This is their opportunity to admire the dexterity with which an epicure carves his lark on the plate, eating each piece of meat as it is detached.

Those epicures can be difficult company. They are very sensitive to the scent of any but the freshest of fruit and they resent the table being stacked with odorous blooms like hyacinth and jasmine (doubtless they also dislike phul-nana and chypre, but there is not much they can do about it). Some of these *bons viveurs* are even "curious or absent-minded enough to examine champagne corks in the houses of those with whose cellars they are not thoroughly acquainted".

Moreover, conversation tends to wither and die in the presence of a gourmet. This problem is tackled most sympathetically and understandingly in *Society Small Talk*. On the way in to dinner the epicure and the lady thrust upon him have worked through the routine exchanges like "When did you come up?" (or "When did you come down?"). He may even have asked her "Do you paint on china?" and have been asked in return "Do you model in soap?"

At the table the lady inquires of her companion, point blank, whether he prefers food to conversation. Appreciating her straightforward approach, he replies "I hope you won't think me quite a bear if I own to a predilection for doing one thing at a time."

This would silence many. But a well-bred lady of spirit comes back with "You are not singular in your choice. There are, I believe, many people who cannot say agreeable things and enjoy the pleasures of the palate at the same moment, and in devoting themselves to one they lose the subtle aroma of the other, which they prefer to 'the feast of reason and the flow of soul'."

The gentleman, tearing his gaze from the *chaudfroids*, protests that his partner is being very severe; after all, he only tried to give her an honest answer. As a gesture he says he will wave away the next course, which consists of sweetbreads. In mock distress the lady protests that he must on no account seek to propitiate her by such an act of self-abnegation, but he insists. Then, when the dish is safely out of the way, he tries to pretend that he never intended to eat sweetbreads, and adds, maliciously, "Let me whisper—a sweetbread is a gland".

Pretending that she did not know this, the lady vows she will become a vegetarian on the spot. The conversational ball is now rolling merrily, the host beams, and the servant removes the unwanted glands. They have served their purpose.

There is another opening by which a lady guest can score off a gourmet and that is by commenting, *à propos* the *pâtés de cailles*, "I think it is very cruel the way these poor little birds are kept alive in flat wooden boxes on view at the poulterers". If he knows his small talk the gentleman will reply with a *tu quoque*, pointing out the miseries endured by those birds which yield up their feathers for feminine headgear. His partner will then be driven to deplore the slaughter of the autumn *battues*, to which the only answer is that a good sportsman cannot do other than offer up his best coverts to his friends. Once again the host beams. The knowledge that his guests know the rules of good small talk makes him feel that all his efforts have been worth while. Yet there are times when he shares the view that the hard rules of precedence create "a compulsory ill-assortment of guests". It would be far better, he thinks, to seat the high-born all together at a separate table (not, of course, a round table), or even on a dais, as one does with a serene highness and his intimates, instead of "sending them down to dinner according to the claims of their ancestors rather than on their own merits".

A host who has only a modest establishment of servants is careful not to employ outdoor men at his dinner table, for the "trail of the serpent," otherwise the odour of the stables, may cling to their persons. If he employs hired servants he makes a point of informing the agency that he wants only spruce young men, not elderly ones. When asked why he dislikes elderly waiters he replies "They have an objectionable habit of wheezing and puffing and breathing hard when pouring out wine". No conscientious host should feel embarrassed at making such stipulations as these. After all, smart young waiters cost no more than slovenly old ones.

The thoughtful host is also careful to ensure that he has a presentable servant to open the door. Unfortunately, he cannot always be aware of the humiliations suffered on his doorstep by respectable callers before the door is opened. As an extreme example, consider the dilemma of a lady who is obliged to travel in a hired carriage without her own footman. Arriving at the house, she faces the problem of ringing the doorbell. If she "desires" the coachman to do so, the fellow may well be reluctant to climb down from his box. Probably he will prefer to hail a passing boy and politely request him to ring the bell, indicating with his whip the door in question. Not all passing boys, however, can be relied upon to respond politely to a request of this kind, and both coachman and passenger may find themselves faced with gratuitous impertinence from a member of the lower orders.

There is a third possible course of action, which not every well-bred lady would care to contemplate; namely, that she should climb out of the carriage and ring the bell for herself. Frankly, one is a little surprised to find "A Member of the Aristocracy" recommending this course. He says that it is sometimes done by "ladies with more sense and less dignity". This is one of the very few occasions when one feels that the author is allowing his better judgment to be impaired by the restless, adventurous spirit of the age.

There are various other forms of hospitality on which advice is offered, notably bachelors' breakfasts (at which it is smarter to serve claret than champagne) and afternoon dances. The latter are not held in London but are a feature of that quaint social life which goes on in the provinces, and are popular with officers of military garrisons. A piano band is adequate for the occasion. For refreshment the hostess need supply only champagne cup, claret cup, tea, coffee, and ices.

Would it not be easier, perhaps, to give a tea party? But a certain amount of trouble must be taken even in making a cup of tea. A careful hostess would not dream of filling the kettle just by holding it under the kitchen tap. The proper water to use is spring water, and failing that river water, or conceivably well water. Tap water is not even mentioned.

"I said 'Push me the sugar'!"

Oh say
Can You See by the
Green Dashboard Light

In which KENNETH ALLSOP paints his
wagon and comes along

REMEMBER how Paul Newman drove that ninety-foot-long convertible in *Hud*? The insolent, spearmint-rotating, quizzical aw-shucks way he lounged sideways in the bench seat, right hand scratching the nape of his neck and tipping his hat forward and left elbow slurped over the door as he rammed down his tooled Marlboro Country boot and sent the four hundred and fifty-four cubic inch V8 engine howling in front of a tornado of white dust?

Wearing that lazy, bitter smile, you should also stop an American auto in the same style. To achieve optimum tyre-scream and body-yaw you watch for an eateria behind a tacky macadam patch. Head lolling on the magenta vinyl trim, a soul cartridge in the stereo-sonic tape system, you swing the car so that it heaves over the soft shoulder, still highballing, and as you nuzzle your king-size miracle filter into the glowing labia of the cigar lighter you pivot your high heel and hit the brake pedal. Powville. This is an extra high, because all American car pedals feel like stepping on to a pontoon plank: they clank soggily underfoot, slopping about in the socket, and delayed seconds later you're yanked to a stop as if an anchor had hooked on an underground granite seam, so that the superstructure lunges ahead of the frame a boat length. When you've got the feel, you can gouge out two inches of smoulding tar, make the short-order cook burn his hamburgers and send the Dow Jones industrial average shuddering ten points out of par.

Of course you wouldn't have been steering with more than four fingers hung flaccidly at noon position on the chartreuse plastic hoop. To turn off your sheet-metal trampoline at speed you spin the wheel like a steam-roller's and barrel forward, lickety-switch, using the three hundred and sixty horsepower like a cowpoke over-riding a newly broken mustang, gunning the motor for that groovy stop.

An Englishman bent on integrating with the Newmanish natives may initially find this hypertense relaxed recklessness incredibly exhausting. For one thing, it's always purple midnight through those wraparound blind bluesman shades you'll be wearing and because of the terrible strain of sloping your eyeballs backward at that round rear mirror jutting like a dislocated shoulder blade above the door handle.

Now I don't mean that Paul came sidling up, hands stuffed in his chinos, kicking heads of daisies, to wheedle tips on how to do it. No, no. Long before I saw *Hud* or had been to America, I knew exactly how to handle an American car. When I first actually slid into the driving seat of a Detroit dream-chariot—a Thunderbird, with sequential turn tail signals, in Los Angeles—my genes transmitted decoded instructions, my blood sang with received conditioning memories which since childhood had fitted me for the fantasy as one born to the chrome brightwork. Before I even turned the ignition key—out there in the far green yonder amid the thickets of pale Bakelite nipples—I had no doubts about how to conduct myself with a Mile-Devouring, Sailplane-Silent Turnpike Master. I hadn't been raised on Andy Hardy films for nothing. Since I was twelve I'd known how you went round in your Plymouth jalopy to call for Ann Rutherford, reading in a swing seat on her white frame house porch, who ran across the unfenced lawn, bobbysox dancing, jumped in by stepping on the door, and then you whooshed away along those glary concrete boulevards with stitches across them for a Coke at the drive-in or to join the other junior high kids for buttermilk waffles with Vermont maple syrup at the Chuck Wagon Soda Fountain on the breezeway and Charlie Barnet on the jukebox. I'd been one of the gang for years.

It's quite surprising how nothing surprises in the United States although all is new. It's all wider-spread, like wind-blown rubbish from a tip; it's more scruffily voluptuous. Fiction becomes fact—or have you become a character in the fiction? Still you feel real at home in the charnel house. Pull yourself up an electric chair and visit a piece, stranger. You already knew from a thousand Odeon features and TV serials that this would be the landscape as you move through the wonderland tollgates and on to the parkways and zipways and skyways, westward from the East Coast shiny shambles into the hinterland of shambolic shininess. Follow your Sunoco "Discover America Best By Car" map through Washington down on to Hiway 95 and across to Route 66 and the frontier myth, now sawn up into sub-divisions for Sunset Retirement Homes for Senior Citizens.

The back projection is the way you saw it through the eyes of *The Fugitive* or *Easy Rider:* beautiful mountain and desert in short gulps between the rain of body blows of electric salesmanship, a continuous carnival of Gulf and Kayo filling stations raving with bunting and blinking signs so excited that the petrol smokes as it's pumped into your tank, while nine men lift out your windscreen and relaminate it, wax polish your coachwork and shampoo your hair. It's a 3,000 mile long Persian market of Broasted Chicken Parlors, Snax, tacos lounges, Midget Mansion Motels, Bide-a-Wee Weddingomats, Home of the Hellhound Hot Dog, Pancakeoriums, banks surrounded by knotty Frontier Fencing with sonic-eye deathray guns trained on the slidedoors, donuts-franks-coffee-burgers, supermart plazas the size of Heathrow, Root Beer 10c, Pumpernik's Sandwich Shoppe, heritage park where 5,000 Pawnees were sanitized by the cavalry, Greyhound Post Houses and orange stalls proud about their Dubl-Juice tree-ripened fruit, Litebite Bakerette for English Muffins, the Holiday Inns and Howard Johnsons and momomomomotels: a linear Disneyland along the "Buffalo Bill Route" of US 30 into the coin-o-matic Wild West.

It's a 9,000 mile round trip worth making if you get through the first twenty-five yards. When I zoomed away on my first solo I drove confidently along the left hand side, speedily closer to an oncoming Viking Freightliner with a zebra-striped bumper, fifty headlamps and two men in the cab waving and hullooing at me with a passionate friendliness which warmed my heart as I swerved, a mite close for comfort, on to the opposite side of the road. I then pressed what I had no reason to suspect was not the electric window button. Silly billy. A faint whirr behind drew my attention to the fact that the hood had risen from its invisible recess to a vertical position, a wagging giant Batman wing. As the car was beginning sluggishly to become airborne like Chitty-Chitty Bang-Bang I pulled in to correct this, laughing heartily at the joshing of the cop who came over and said in that high-pitched strangulated rasp with which they entertain students (part of President Nixon's turn-a-new-leaf "Buddy-up With A Campus Bum" campaign): "Watsa madda, mac, you cold or somethin'?" as he gazed with haddock eyes at my vertical sheet of buckled canvas.

On successive driving visits I came to understand better the nuances of road-piggery (never give a sucker an even break; never look at another motorist; stare through them and if necessary drive through them) but the fascination never fades of being cast for a part in the great, wide-screen saga of American life, two hundred million Huck Finns lighting out for the territories. (They bulldozed the territories flat for a Manned Spacecraft Centre and a training base for Green Beret gunghos soon to be needed for invading Australia and the Communist-infested Parrot's Beak of the Tasmanian Isthmus.) You'll meet them all—but it's not all multi-lane dual carriageways. The Interstate Highway System has to date cost thirty-three billion dollars (most of which was won in a Little Rock dice game by a consortium of Sicilian lasagna-importers) and is still only two-thirds completed. So far the US has spent more trying to reach California than it did reaching the moon. That's what the Loneliest Man of Destiny in the World, Richard Nixon, broods about when he strolls around all night, a wee bit min, down at his San Clemente hideyhole, whistling mournfully "Drop Me Off At Bedlam" (a tune he once heard a jigaboo called Ellington playing) before consoling himself with a corned beef hash breakfast.

To be fair, I'm a bit out of touch with how it is over on Death's bowling alleys (seventy per cent more fatalities on the roads than inflicted by the Viet Cong; total number of Americans killed in crashes more than in all the nation's wars). After the demonsterisation of Nixon, the demonsterisation of the juggernaut: the megamotors are being slugged to bits by the sub-compacts, indistinguishable in size. Would I know where I was with the Oldsmobile Cutlass and Plymouth Barracuda? There's the disorientating news that this year's Chevrolet Monte Carlo has only single headlights, against the stupefying great leap forward of double pairs a year or two back. This is one tactic to lick the sensational smally, the Hornet, which has achieved the quint-essential is-ness of a perfect door-closing *thunk*. For years the auto industry has been trying to orchestrate the ineffable *thunk*, and it had to be found by a cheapskate made in Kenosna, Wisconsin.

If you see people going round their car at restaurants repeatedly slamming the doors, saying "I think that thunked okay," you'll know you're in Hornet country. Let's hope that every Briton who won't accept that nothing can take longer than getting down the Exeter by-pass, and insists on adding to the four hundred billion miles of tyre travel Americans clock up annually, will love every neon-lit mile and every stop at Dittoville. You may be only just in time. The Americans are rising in wrath against the tyrant car. During Earth Day a group of young anti-pollution crusaders ritually buried a model brand new from Satan's spanner. After the demo, they all piled into their cars and caroomed away in blue vapour. Well, they had to get back for the Peace Rally battle with the National Guard, hadn't they? Any more for the monorail?

"I've got a three-litre Rover at the moment about a mile outside Salford."

Drinking Songs for Very Rich Men

PETER DICKINSON

WINE AND/OR WOMEN

Woman, as every schoolboy knows,
  Assorts but ill with wine.
Her cheek may be the scented rose,
  Her embonpoint divine.
    (Far gone, far gone the diner able
    To see much more—beneath the table.)
But oh, the odour of that rose,
  The heaving of that chest,
Confounds the senses, fills the nose—
  What wine can stand the test?
    I learned this wisdom from my father
      Who told me, nothing loth,
    "Enjoy whichever you would rather
      But don't, my son, try both."
Love of good wine, each housewife knows,
  Is not so good for love.
How often does some lad propose
  Some lassie's worth to prove
    (Selecting her because the wine
    Has somehow made the wit resign.)
But she, when tempted to his cell
  With maidenly demur,
Finds he who does himself too well
  Does not so well with her.
    I learned this wisdom from my granny:
      "They both are worth the bother,
    But if you'd be a Man, my mannie,
      You must choose one or other."

Now we, as all assembled know,
  Have made a useful hoard
And rare indeed is the Chateau,
  Or girl, we can't afford.
    But still we face this problem which
    Afflicts the poor man and the rich.
Let us resignedly carouse,
  Forgetting love's delight.
This is the night, my friends, to souse—
  To-morrow's Ladies' Night.
    I learned this wisdom from my mother:
      I teach it to my sons:
    "Choose sometimes one and sometimes t'other,
      But never both at once."

THE THREE OLD MEN

I'll sing you a song of a rich old man
Who (poor old man) put a total ban
  On liquor, but being wealthy
He spent an enormous amount of dough
In search for the purest H_2O.
  He found it. It tasted filthy.
CHORUS: He wasn't our sort like we're our sort.
        Bring on the dancing girls! Pass the port!

    I'll sing you a song of a rich old man
    Who (poor old man) was a puritan.
      His notion of wicked living
    Was owning a great pink Renoir nude
    Which once a year he unveiled and viewed
      With a sort of baffled misgiving.
    CHORUS: He wasn't our sort like we're our sort.
            Bring on the dancing girls! Pass the port!

I'll sing you a song of a rich old man
Who (poor old man) was a health-food fan.
  The victuals upon his table
Were brown bread baked from a hand-milled wheat
From a humus farm—and of that he'd eat
  As little as he was able.
CHORUS: He wasn't our sort like we're our sort.
        Bring on the dancing girls! Pass the port!

    Now these three old fellows they all went bust
    Through choosing the wrong companions to trust.
      (Have I mentioned they weren't our sort?)
    We've solved that problem with minimum fuss,
    For none of us trust any of us,
      Except to pass the port.
    CHORUS: For you are my sort like I'm your sort.
            Bring on the dancing girls! Pass the port!

*"Honestly, Dad, I don't think I could
manage another bitter lemon."*

OLD CITY TOAST

Here's a health unto the Chancellor
  (with a fal fiddle lal and whistle for a wind)
Who brings new notions by the score
To rescue the Economee
And foists them on the Treasuree
  (with a fal fiddle lal and whistle for a wind)

Here's a health unto the Treasuree
  (with a ho hum hum and wait another year)
They've dealt before with such as hee.
They tell him that it can't be done
And pray that soon he will be gone.
  (with a ho hum hum and wait another year)

Here's a health to him and a health to them
  (with a rum dumble dum and what's in it for me)
If they leave in peace poor businessmen.
May the Chancellor soon be made a Lord
And the Civil Servant sit on our board.
  (with a rum dumble dum and what's in it for me)

"One day, son, a little of this will be yours."

On the Eating of Asparagus

THERE were twenty-three ways of eating asparagus known to the ancients. Of these the best-known method was to suspend it on pullies about three feet from the ground and "approach the green" on one's back along the floor; but it was discontinued about the middle of the fourth century, and no new method worthy of serious consideration was subsequently evolved, till the August or September of 1875, when a Mr. Gunter-Brown wrote a letter to the A.A.R. ("The Asparagus Absorbers' Review and Gross Feeders' Gazette"), saying that he had patented a scheme more cleanly and less unsightly than the practice of tilting the head backward at an angle of forty-five degrees and lowering the asparagus into the expectant face, which is shown by statistics to have been the mode usually adopted at that time.

Mr. Gunter-Brown's apparatus, necessary to the method he advocated, consisted of a silver or plated tube, into which each branch of asparagus, except the last inch, was placed, and so drawn into the mouth by suction, the eater grasping the last uneatable inch, together with the butt end of the tube, in the palm of his hand. Asparagus branches being of variable girth, a rubber washer inserted in the end of the tube furthest from the eater's mouth helped to cause a vacuum.

The inventor claimed that the edible portion of the delicacy became detached if the intake of the eater was strong enough, but he overlooked the fact that the necessary force caused the asparagus to pass through the epiglottis into the oesophagus before the eater had time to enjoy the taste (as was proved by experiment) and so all sense of pleasure was lost.

More prospective marriages have been marred through the abuse of asparagus at table than through mixed bathing at Tunbridge Wells. For instance, though the matter was hushed up at the time, it is an open secret among their friends that Miss Gladys Devereux broke off her engagement to young Percy Gore-Mont on account of his gaucherie when assimilating this weed at a dinner-party. It seems that he simply threw himself at the stuff, and that one of the servants had to comb the melted butter out of his hair before he could appear in the drawing-room.

The case of the Timminses, too, presents very sad features, though the marriage was not in this case abandoned, the high contracting parties not having once encountered a dish of asparagus simultaneously during the engagement. Yet it is more than rumoured that when, at the end of the close season, asparagus may be hunted, there is considerable friction in the Timminses' household, because Mrs. Timmins plays with a straight fork, while Timmins affects the crouching style.

Happily, however, a light at last appears to be shining through the darkness. Under the auspices of the Vegetable Growers' Association (Luxury Trades section) an asparagus-eating contest has been arranged to take place in the Floral Hall early in July. As the entrants to date include a contortionist and at least three well-known war-profiteers, it is confidently expected that some startling methods will be exhibited which may revolutionise asparagus-eating in this country.

Club Attendant (to stout party, who is struggling into overcoat). "Allow me, Sir,"
Stout Party. "No, don't trouble! This is the only exercise I ever take!"

Oh Come All Ye Trendy

ALAN COREN

"Mr. Noble has no doubts about the civilised way to drink at Christmas. 'A long glass of ice-cold champagne in my bath. It's expensive—66s. 6d. a bottle. When people come in for drinks, I shall offer them a pétillante Blanquette de Limoux, at 25s. 3d.'"   *Harpers Bazaar*

"This year, why not a whole roast ox?"   *Esquire*

"We always give our parties a topical theme, and dress and act accordingly. This Christmas it's going to be Student Rebellion."   *American Home*

WELL, Mr. Noble, we've come a long way from the manger, you and I. I have it on irreproachable authority that it would have been possible to go through Bethlehem with a fine-toothed comb a mere 1969 years ago and still not have come up with more than a handful of citizens who were drinking champagne in the bath. It's not taken long to get us civilised, all things considered.

Not, however, that your own plans for a fun-filled Yule leave nothing to be desired. I have no objections to your mounting your Christmas thrash among the perspiring tiles, chacun à son wassail, but it strikes me as something less than hospitable to retire to the suds with three gnsworth of vintage bubbles, leaving your guests with only a *pétillante* Blanquette de Limoux to take the enamel off their teeth. For readers currently too dazed by this glimpse of la dolce Christmas to grope for their Harrap's Shorter French, *pétillante* comes from *péter*, to break wind, and 25s. 3d. derives from the English *cheap*. Now that you've broken the story in *Harpers*, my personal advice would be to shelve all thought of a Christmas binge and see the season out in some quiet Eastbourne retreat, twelve quid all-in, including free cracker and choice of mince pie or nut. Trendy it ain't, but it's safer than being nudely besieged among your own porcelain by a platoon of enraged Blanquette drinkers, incensed by the song of a popping cork behind the bathroom door.

The question posed by *Esquire* will be fraught with unanswerability for those readers whose demented efforts to separate a small turkey from one or other of its extremities has resulted in a turnup full of stuffing and a slashed jugular. For such scarred and apprehensive carvers, the thought of matching wits with a whole roast ox revolving sneakily on its spit will leave the brain ringing and the palms clammy. Especially since the aforementioned whole roast item is considerably larger than the average dining recess and the net result of trying to feed off it would leave most families smaller by two or three spitted children, not to mention the odd elderly relative crackling in the flames and casting a pall both literal and metaphorical over the entire Noël. Bedsitter-dwellers seduced, in spite of all this, by the *Esquire* offer, would be well-advised to start small and work up; a whole roast mouse, say, would bring a touch of *ton* to your solitary proceedings. It's hell to stuff, of course, but it turns a treat on a knitting-needle. Forty minutes on a low candle, and don't forget to baste.

That's the trouble with Christmas among the glossy set. As with anything else for which life is worth living, Lamborghinis and chinchillas and emerald tooth-stoppings, fierceness of competition is the bugbear, the coloured person in the woodpile. Up here among us trendies, it's Christmas red in tooth and claw, friends, and don't you forget it: how can we help one another, this Christmas, to make the world a more envious, greedy place, and knock spots off the finks in the neo-Gothic penthouse opposite? It's not the thought, it's the gift in front of it. Leafing through the shimmering pages of *Queen* in search of something for the little woman, as well as a present for my wife, I find such uplifting sales-pitches as "Christmas at Cartier begins at £50," a message calculated to bring cheapjacks sprinting from all over the realm in search of stocking-fodder. It's "Where Christmas Starts" *apud* the Cartier copywriters, and who will say them nay?

"By Jove—that was a narrow escape."

There's a hard time ahead for us pace-setters, I don't mind telling you, and a glance at the harrowed faces moping along Beauchamp Place and South Audley Street will bear instant witness to the hell of trying to keep up with, and preferably get ahead of, the Harpers. Noble's bath booze-up, for example, is so old-hat, it's not true: this year, my wife and I are throwing our first party on Christmas Eve, before anyone pinches our idea of filling our swimming-pool with prephylloxera Mouton Cadet and chucking our guests in at the deep end to guzzle their way through to midnight. Anyone failing to bring his or her sable bath-towel will be forced to drink in the paddling-pool with the kiddies, and no second helpings on the quail patties!

Christmas Day, of course, we shall be having the traditional dinner, an old-fashioned family do, just a few pages of *Burke's Peerage* invited at random, with a Redgrave or two to pass round the paper hats. We've hit on rather a splendid main course, we think: why, of the two traditional Christmas animals, should it always be a whole roast ox that everyone eats? This year, we're having a whole roast ass. We're getting round the problem of carving by taking as our Christmas Day party theme the Pleistocene Era: everyone's coming in Mister Fish okapi-skins, and we're just going to tear bits off the ass and gnaw them in the time-honoured way. It may not be topical, but we did Vietnam for our Hallowe'en Ball and Biafra for Poppy's coming-out thing, and one tends to run out of newsy motifs, doesn't one? After dinner, all the chaps chuck their clubs in a heap, and the wives have to pick a club and go off with the owner; it's going to be an absolute hoot! Apicella designed our caves specially.

Boxing Day's always a problem, isn't it? It's partly the inevitable feeling of anti-climax, partly the irksome task of initiating divorce proceedings, but mainly it's the money. There never seems anything left to spend it on. Still, we've come up with rather a good wheeze this year—we've hired Cardiff Arms Park for the merest of king's ransoms, and we're taking as our theme the Springbok tour. It's a Boutiquiers XV against the Frost Script-writers Second Team, kick-off 3.15, floodlights by Cartier and half-time lemons by the Clement Freud Citrus Ensemble. Of course, we're frightfully nervous that the whole thing will turn out an utter shambles: it's Snowdon's first time as a referee, and since his entire sporting life to date seems to have been coxing the Cambridge boat, there's every likelihood that the game will end up with both scrums running backwards up the A40 at thirty-two strokes per minute and going like the clappers for Putney Bridge. Still, we've hired the South Wales Constabulary to drag guests off to the nick, so there should be something for everyone.

We've not forgotten the kiddies, either. After a *pétillante* gripewater cup at Alvaro's, they're all off to Holland Park Comprehensive for Ken's super new nativity romp, *Oh!*

Bethlehem! Then it's back to Tiberio's for the gala **Rusk And Gerbers Fork Supper**, leaving nanny with an hour or two to herself to thank daddy properly for the monogrammed underwear.

Saturday, of course, we're holding our Mini-Moke Rally, starting off with mulled vodka at Kenny Palace and ending up with tobogganing on Harrod's Simulated Snow Slope and a refreshing mixed sauna at David Morgan's, before settling down again to roast something whole in time for our al fresco party on Hampstead Heath. The theme is the Normandy Landings, by the way, in case you're from ITN, or know anyone who might be.

Which leaves only Sunday to be got rid of. Sunday's the most terrible day of all, really, because that's when all the Supplements come, and you have to go through them, heart banging away like a trip-hammer—they'll all be doing their post-Christmas stuff, you see, and sure as God made little green banknotes, you're bound to find that someone's been doing something you didn't, something more In, something more Now. That's the worst about Christmas—with all the effort and all the excitement and all the beastly in-fighting and everything, you often come to the end of it all only to find that you've completely overlooked something terribly, terribly important.

"'What!' I said indignantly, 'you expect me, a ten pound a week clerk married with seven children living in a nice council flat seventeen storeys up, to commit this vile act of industrial sabotage.' I said . . ."

"Bring another duck, waiter."

THE PUDDING MAN

ROBERT MORLEY

I AM a pudding man. Nothing depresses me more than a meal which doesn't finish with one. "Just coffee for me, thanks," is not a phrase in my book. However boring the occasion, I perk up when they wheel in the sweet trolley. I inspect it as I would a guard of honour. I insist the jellies should be standing to attention, the rhubarb, although I never touch it, pale pink, the chocolate sauce dark and mysterious. I cannot contemplate a spoilt trifle. "What was in that?" I ask, as I wave away the half-filled dish and wait for the replacement. Sometimes there are several trolleys going the rounds. It is as well to inspect them all. They are seldom identical. The first lesson I taught my children was never to show your hand when being served from a trolley. Never ask for a little of that and a little of that, please. If you have decided on profiteroles and syllabub, encourage the waiter to pile your plate with the former, and only when he has put back the spoon, suddenly, and on the spur of the fork, as it were, demand the syllabub.

Because I am a great artist myself, I know the disappointment of rejection. I know what it is like to "bang on the slap" and find the house empty. I know what it must be like for a chef to send out a Creme Honore and have it returned untouched. When no one bought his paintings, Gauguin, or was it Van Gogh, cut off his own ear. A kitchen is full of knives. I must put no similar temptation in the way of a pastrycook.

I look forward to the petit fours, often nibbling the spun sugar in the swan's beak, or breaking off a piece of the basket and chewing the wicker work. I am not fond of marzipan. It is not a medium in which a chef does his finest work. The best sweet trolleys are always to be found in Italian restaurants, the most meagre in Indian ones. The two finest puddings I have ever tasted are the circular mille feuilles obtainable at the Chateau de Madrid and an Orange Boodle Fool my daughter occasionally makes at the weekends when we have company.

I am a lifelong enemy of tapioca, but every now and then am seduced by a prune. I am still fond of a good meringue, but never hope to taste again quite the perfection of my grandmother's. I was smaller in those days, but a meringue should always be judged like a vegetable marrow, by its size.

I was once thrashed by a schoolmaster for insisting that fried bread spread with jam was not a pudding at all, and refusing to leave my place at the dining table until the mistake had been rectified. Naturally, it never was. Mind you, I like fried bread at breakfast, but not, of course, spread with jam. I am not an American, thank God.

Of the rest of my schooldays I remember with pleasure only the tuck shop on the days I could afford a tenpenny mess (one banana, two scoops ice-cream and extra cream). I don't say I was happy then, but I was a little less miserable. While others dreamt of success on the playing fields, my private fantasy was a box of milk flake bars to myself.

For a time after I left school I was hooked on Walnut Whips, but ever afterwards have been a milk chocolate addict. I share my craving with one of my own cats. Together we prowl the house, searching for the cache where my wife has hidden the bars she buys for the children. When we discover the hoard, we demolish it. Naturally, my share is larger than Tom's, but once we have awoken our taste buds, nothing can stop us. I have even known Tom to eat the silver paper. I have left many things unfinished in my life, but never a bar of chocolate. I haven't a wisdom tooth in my head, but thank the Lord I still have a sweet one.

THE TAX GAME

This quiz is designed so that you start out with the maximum score which is reduced as you go along. You are a company chief with 100 points (pre-tax), intent on keeping as many as possible intact. *Punch* is the Inland Revenue, determined to strip you of as much profit as is inhumanly possible. Now fight on.

---

1. Have you already contacted a skilled accountant to manage this quiz for you? Deduct 5 points if you have not—add 5 points if you got an ex-Revenue man to take over the answering, but only if he immediately advised you not to mention the extra 5 points to anyone.

---

2. Why, in your tax returns, have you not mentioned the profits of your subsidiary in Dutch Guiana? Don't you know this is a serious offence?
(a) "I'm terribly sorry, I've no idea how it happened." (You lose all your points. You'll never make a good tobacconist, let alone a good tycoon.)
(b) "I think you'll find it all included in our returns for Guyana." (Not bad. It won't be, of course, but you should have thought of something else by then. Deduct 2 points.)
(c) "We are still negotiating with the Dutch tax office—we wanted to be sure of our figures there before we filed with you." (Good, good. Make a memo to get in touch with the Dutch tax people at once and deduct 1 point for lying.)
(d) "Dutch Guiana has been paralysed for the last seven months by a postal strike and the figures are aboard a Liberian tanker which is, according to our information, having trouble with its stabilisers." (Add 5 points for initiative. Deduct 5 points for smiling as you say it.)

---

3. How do you explain this item about grouse-shooting in Scotland?
(a) "Well, as some of us go shooting anyway in the autumn, we thought we'd try and claim it against tax." (Look, you were thrown out of this quiz in the last question. You don't get your points back now, you know.)
(b) "We have organised a new recreational area in Perthshire where members of the firm, at the firm's expense, can take an active holiday pursuing old Scottish sports. At the moment it is limited to executives but we hope to extend it very soon." (The only possible answer. Deduct 2 points.)

---

4. We don't understand your claims concerning French lessons for members of the company. Could you clarify?
(a) "Mais c'est assez simple si vous comprenez le système qu'on a employé ci-dessous." (Good try, but all our quiz staff are multilingual. Get on with it.)

(b) "As part of the export drive, we have installed mobile French laboratories for all executive staff, and we feel that this expense should be allowed to us for patriotic reasons." (What you mean is that all executive cars have now been fitted with stereophonic systems and umpteen cassettes of Sacha Distel and Edith Piaf. Deduct 1 point, but if we find you've claimed for the cars elsewhere again, it will be 10 and no appeal.)

(c) "We arrange for select members of the staff to take refresher language fortnights in Paris every year." (Not that old chestnut! Deduct 10 points.)

(d) "We arrange for select members of the staff to take refresher courses every year in the suburbs of Clermont-Ferrand." (That's more like it. Suggestions of hardship do impress us, you know. Deduct 5 points.)

---

5. Have you any objection to us arbitrarily deducting 40 points?

(a) "Not if you allow us the following seventy-five claims . . ." (Good bargaining. You get the 40 points back.)

(b) "No." (That was too glib by half. We've missed some fiddle or other, haven't we? Take your 40 points back while we go and look for it.)

---

6. According to our assessment of Corporation Tax, including consideration of "fair market value" and so on, you now lose 43½ points. According to your assessment you only lose 36⅔ points. Where do we go from here?

(a) "We suggest revising your reinterpretation of excess profits by 2¾ points, lowering short-term figures by 8¾, adjusting land value assessments by 7⅓, revising . . ." (All right, all right. But you realise we aren't going to get this quiz finished before 1973?)

(b) "Shall we toss a coin?" (Fair enough. Remember to claim it as a legitimate expense.)

---

7. Why haven't you tried charging the time spent on this instructional quiz against tax?

(a) "We did not think it would qualify as tax deductible." (What on earth has that got to do with it? Claim first, find out afterwards. Deduct 8 points. No, 15 points.)

(b) "We are waiting till it is finished. No sense in claiming on half a quiz." (Actually, we won't allow the claim. Deduct 5 points.)

---

8. Why are you and your accountant whispering like that?

(a) "We are working out the implications of the four new financial acts which have been passed since this quiz started." (Really? We shall call an emergency lunch break for the same purpose. Add 5 points.)

(b) "We are forming a new company to make a take-over bid for this quiz." (Sorry, we are gone to lunch.)

9. What are you going to do with us, now that you own us?
(a) "Cut out all this writing, have lots more sports coverage and get some pretty girls in."
(b) "Pull you down and put up a vast new shopping centre."
10. Can we announce the results before we collect our hats and coats?
(a) "Yes, but hurry up. This isn't a charitable organisation, you know."

Results: 15 points or under, you will be taken over or go bankrupt soon. 15 to 40 points, not bad but you must lie harder. 40 to 60 points, we will use our golden handshake to buy shares in you. Over 60 points, a new finance act will be passed any moment to deal with you. We would like to take this opportunity of thanking all our quiz-answerers for their past custom and patronage.

"I still reckon we should 'ave been the 8.35 to the City."

Wine, Women, No Song

B. A. YOUNG

Wine-tasting is not quite the same thing as wine-drinking, and a slightly different code of deportment is required. Here are a few notes for beginners.

THERE are proverbially five reasons why men drink, into which I don't propose to go at the moment (any good dealer in poker-work mottoes can supply them); but only three of them apply to wine-tasting. The two to be excluded are "being dry" and "lest we should be by and by"; anyone who goes to a wine-tasting with a roaring thirst is heading for trouble. The object of a wine-tasting is not to put the stuff away but to assess the relative values of a varied assortment of bottles. It should thus rate high as a civilized exercise with devotees of Dean Swift, who made Gulliver explain to the Houyhnhnms as a token of our culture that "we ate when we were not hungry and drank without the provocation of thirst".

Tyros who jog elbows with notable connoisseurs as they pick up the art of tasting should not, however, go away with the idea that the wine-tasting code always applies when drinking for culture rather than for pleasure. Because it is *de rigueur* at a tasting to roll your drink around your mouth, soak your tongue in it, and then spit it out into a bin of sawdust, there is no need to do the same with your dry Martini at the reception for Marlene Garbo at the Barchester, and, in fact, if you do so you may easily cause several smartly-dressed women to sweep out with expressions of disdain. On the other hand, if those same women swallowed their wine at a tasting with the same avidity as their gin at the Barchester, they would run a considerable risk of themselves being swept out, probably with an expression of dismay.

Before even beginning to take part, the visitor to a wine-tasting must find out (if he doesn't know) who his host is, and which of the others present matter. There is no disguising the fact that the sight of a row of oenophiles sniffing their wine, twiddling it round in their glasses, examining it for the presence of goldfish, stroking it, setting fire to it, anything in the world except drinking it, can be a very daunting one. Anyone who feels like being daunted by it should just go right ahead. The man who, having got rid of his hat and coat, takes one look at the company and, slapping the nearest back, announces "Hundred to six I get round before any of those squares," only to find that the back belongs to the founder of the feast, is not likely to see himself on the invitation list another time.

The actual process of tasting the wine is very simple. To quote from an erudite little essay entitled *The Future of Expectoration*, by Mr. Guy Prince, who has done so much to raise wine-tasting to the level of a national sport, "To taste wine you must first try its bouquet . . . then roll it round your palate so that the taste-buds do their work, then you must form your opinion, and finally *you must spit it out.*"

It will readily be seen that only men and women of quick judgment are likely to be a social success at this game. If it takes you several minutes to make up your mind about a wine, the company is likely to be deprived of your conversation for a long time as you gaze anxiously around the cellar, your taste-buds awash, your lips sealed.

In an emergency it is sometimes better to have some ready-made opinions available so that you can empty your mouth and reply to some pressing question, such as "What do you think of the new Eliot play?" without interposing an embarrassing silence. Opinions about wine are notoriously as ambiguous as the utterances of the Delphic oracle, and a few handy words such as "acceptable," "interesting," "restrained," and so on, will generally see you through.

There is no need to emphasize one's judgments by the use of such phrases as "Wow," "Yum yum" or "Phew".

This matter of spitting is one which may be said, at the risk of a little ambiguity, to be coming increasingly into the public eye. At Messrs. Lebègue's tasting this week, Guy Prince has established a school of expectoration, aimed mainly at lady tasters, where the gentle art will be demonstrated by the greatest masters in the land. One remembers Sapper's character who, desiring to tell a French peasant that he had crashed an aeroplane into a field of onions, could get no nearer than *"Nous avons craché dans les rognons."* The point of impact of the ejected wine is not important from the tasting point of view; but from the purely social angle it is advisable to use the sawdust-filled troughs provided and to avoid the floor or the kidneys of fellow-guests.

A point upon which wine impresarios (one can hardly think of such men merely as merchants) are adamant is that you cannot hope to form an unclouded judgment on a wine if you reek of *Cuir de Russie* or Roses of Ispahan after-shave tonic lotion (for men). This is no disparagement of those noble scents, only the recognition of the inescapable fact that they do not blend particularly well with Château Margaux or Domaine de la Romanée-Conti. You wouldn't nibble at *pâté de foie gras* while making mad, passionate love; there are luxuries in this world that demand the stage to themselves. I have seen a man arrive at a wine-tasting with after-shave still glistening on his chin. He was aware of the solecism: "Don't worry, old boy," he said, clapping his host across the shoulders, "I'll drown it in a minute." From his side-pockets he took a tobacco-pouch and an enormous pipe . . .

One final word of warning. Keep your eye on the wine. There was once a tyro wine-taster who found himself standing beside a world-famous connoisseur in front of a bottle of a burgundy of legendary excellence. Nervous but composed, conscious all the time of the expert eye on the back of his neck, he poured himself a sample, imbibed it, rolled it round his tongue, breathed out heavily through his nose while he tried to think of a suitable comment, spat it out, and took a sliver of cheese, courteously provided by the management, to clear his palate. Turning at last to the connoisseur, "What a smashing bit of Gruyère!" he said.

Wine-tasting, in the classic phrase, is a diverting pastime for young and old, for ladies as well as men. It is not so intellectual as chamber-music, it is not so light-hearted as strip-tease; no one will burst out into *"Ach, du lieber Augustin"* as he waves his tiny libation of some promising new vintage around his head, nor will anyone entangle you with problems that need an intimate understanding of Einstein and a slide-rule to answer. It is, in fact, the ideal pursuit with which to while away those idle hours between eleven in the morning and four in the afternoon.

It also, of course, leads in the long run to a wider knowledge of wine.

"It's a great library—they all contain bottles."

Yesterday's Money
WILLIAM DAVIS

MRS. JACQUELINE ONASSIS, it was reported the other day, has only $5,200 in her bank account. "But then," a friend wondered, "how do you live?" Said Jackie: "I just charge everything to Olympic Airways."

Olympic Airways, which happens to be owned by hubby, is not so obliging to everyone, but the episode underlines a fact which is becoming increasingly obvious: cash is out of date.

Government officials may claim that D-day, February 15, will bring "a revolution in our money habits," but the rest of us know that the revolution has happened already. It is difficult to get excited about small change when our whole thinking about the shape and future of money has undergone a profound transformation.

This transformation is, of course, most apparent in the United States. It was an American who, not long ago, described money as "the poor man's credit card," and he wasn't just trying to be funny. Money, in the old-fashioned sense of coins and notes, has ceased to be a status symbol. On the contrary, people who insist on settling bills in cash are increasingly regarded with suspicion: they look like have-nots who cannot be trusted with charge accounts and credit cards.

One does not need a wallet full of banknotes these days to travel around the US. Indeed, it is advisable—because it's safer—to leave it at home. Stores, hotels, supermarkets, petrol stations, car hire firms, restaurants, airlines and many others have all got away from paper money. Even ambulance services and mortuaries take credit cards, and there's a sign outside a San Francisco church which proclaims that your card is good for the collection plate. If it were not for the tiresome necessity of tipping doormen and cab drivers, America would be closer still to fulfilment of the ultimate dream: a cashless society.

Here in Britain we have been somewhat slower to change our ways, but no one would dispute that things are not what they were. The banks, which used to be so stuffy, nowadays behave in a manner which would have been quite unthinkable a decade or two ago. My local off-licence, for example, has given a corner over to dishy Barclay-blondes in yellow Batman cloaks who pounce upon unsuspecting customers, a welcoming glass of Spanish Burgundy in one hand and a free Barclay-card in the other.

There are experts in Britain who believe that, by the end of the century, we may be able to dispense with coins and banknotes altogether. This may strike you as far-fetched, but if you look at the changes in attitudes—and customs—over the past thirty years it seems by no means impossible that cash will eventually become obsolete.

"Money can't buy them happiness."

It is already feasible, if you are so minded, to live without ever touching a single pound note. The cheque has long ceased to be a novelty, even among the working class, and the stigma once attached to borrowing has gone for good. Anyone who suggested, today, that hire-purchase is immoral would be dismissed as a crank.

The wage packet still exists, but millions now have their earnings paid directly into a bank. Luncheon vouchers have been popular for years, and expense account living merely requires a signature. Travellers' cheques are as widely used as season tickets and air travel cards. In short, one can get by on book-keeping transactions.

Government and industry, of course, do so already. And it isn't in the least surprising that, at the international level, the argument over "liquidity" ended in the creation of credits which are accepted as a modern, intelligent substitute for gold and paper cash.

There is no doubt that we shall travel further along this road. The process will be hastened by inflation, as it has been already. As money buys less and less, the conventional coinage and currency will seem more and more inappropriate. The farthing, the ha'penny, and the threepence have already disappeared. How long will it be, do you think, before the Decimal Currency Board's shining new coins will follow?

Handling currency is expensive, time-consuming, and unhygienic. The printing of notes and the manufacture of coin involves considerable cost. So does the elaborate business of moving it around the country with the constant necessity of counting it, packing it, and protecting it. Theoretically, there is no need for any of this. All that matters is that people should be ready and willing to accept whatever form of payment is in fashion. It's not the money as such that counts, but what it will buy.

Almost everything reasonably durable has served as money at one time or another. Iron bars, spears, knives, mother-of-pearl, fishhooks, pieces of silk and copper wire, cowrie shells, and lumps of jade have all been used as cash. Bricks of tea mixed with herbs and bullock's blood were exchanged in Asia until a comparatively short time ago.

In Germany, just after the last war, barter more or less replaced coins and bits of paper. Confidence in them broke down so completely that the country went, in effect, on to the "chocolate standard." Chocolate bars, packets of cigarettes, and tins of coffee were the generally accepted medium of exchange. They passed from hand to hand, just as paper money had done before. I happened to be there at the time and I well remember the reverence in which I—a young boy—held a chocolate bar. It never occurred to me that it had originally been made for eating: in my eyes, it was money.

I am not suggesting that we shall ever reach that stage, though inflation on the scale we have experienced in the past year or two is bound to increase the relative attraction of things like property, jewellery and antiques. What I am saying is that there is, fundamentally, no reason why we should not adopt a system in which currency, as such, plays no significant role. The Decimal Currency Board is making a lot of fuss over something which is about as relevant to the computer age as gas light and steam locomotives.

Our Restaurants

Wife. *"What a lot of money! Do you mean to say the bill came to all that?"*

Husband. *"I've paid the bill. This is the ten-per-cent tip."*

Oh, You've Got That, Too

BEING neither dog nor zoologist, I've no idea what it may be that makes the former decide, after an anal sniff or two whether to wag the tail or fly at the throat. In the case of British dogs, however, I suspect it must be a canine equivalent of the various means by which we, as a race, calculate each other's social weight.

Dogs have keen noses and we have not. Scent therefore, whatever the telly commercials may imply, is no help. At one time we relied mainly on our ears but in the last decade, with the spread of the classless accent, ears have given precedence to eyes. It's no longer the fact you call it the toilet that matters (after all that may be the fruit of an agonised but closely reasoned decision arrived at to avoid confusing the children returning home from their smart State schools), what counts now is the geegaws you hang on its walls, and the same is true of every room in the house. A sniff at each other's decor helps to establish whether our hosts are, in old-fashioned terminology, "our sort" or, to use the more evasive modern nomenclature, "a drag". Sniff, sniff? Grr!

There are signs, however, that even this system is less reliable than it was. The elevation of kitsch and camp has helped confuse the picture. We can no longer be certain we've got it right. "Ha, ha, ha" we may laugh behind the backs of our departing guests, "judging by that look she gave him they obviously thought our collection of chipped plaster ballroom dancers were for real," but how can we be absolutely certain that they may not have rejected us on the grounds that in their book thirties plaster is already old hat?

Is there no way then to establish a social pecking order? Are we to be reduced to actually judging people on their own merits? Not at all. There remains one perfectly reliable

GEORGE MELLY runs a revealing finger along your record shelf

barometer; the LP collection, and what's more there is no need to be coy in reading it. For just as dogs are fools enough to actually present their bottoms for possibly painful evaluation, people expect you to riffle through their records, and to do so isn't in any way considered the equivalent of trying to read a letter upside down, but more like taking advantage of the now discredited come-on of lining up smart invitations along the mantel-shelf.

It's true that LPmanship is still in its infancy, that the definitive thesis has yet to be written, but this makes it easier to rely on. The ambiguous decadence which has crept in to bedevil our competitive decors is still absent. The rules are easy to grasp, the pretenders to unmask. I hope, therefore, that a few interim observations, however fragmentary, may prove useful. Naturally, like all pioneers in the field of the new snobbery, I expect no thanks. The great Miss Mitford herself suffered harshly for her courage and yet who, in the dear dead 'fifties, did more to keep what its defenders call "the rich diversity of English society" alive. Gladly it is with this aim in view that I offer my own modest observations.

THE PRESENTATION

As long as it's more than thirty or so, it doesn't matter how many LPs you have. In fact to display too many is a mistake, suggesting that other areas of life, holidays abroad or campari, etc., may have been sacrificed to what should ideally be thought of as a marginal though essential proof of Colour Mag living. Above all give no sign of having any idea as to how many you've got. LPs should give the impression of having grown of their own mysterious volition like mushrooms.

Although special shelves may be used to house LPs, they shouldn't be too tidy. It is for instance a very bad sign to arrange the records alphabetically, and even worse to divide them into rigid categories, for not only does this reinforce the idea that you care too much, it also prevents guests from establishing your catholic if faultlessly casual taste by flicking through a random sampling. Even so, in order to avoid their suspicion that you may have ordered your records by the yard, as interior decorators do books, it is as well to give evidence that at least once some kind of effort was made to get them into approximate order. On the higher shelves particularly, as many as six LPs in the same genre may lie next to each other, but even at gramophone level one or two may rub sleeves. Any snide reference to order in this context may be countered by an explanation (preferably supplied by your partner), that it was the fruit of some temporary form of neurotic anxiety since overcome.

As to what machine your LPs should be played on, too large a hi-fi system yet again carries a suggestion of enthusiasm in the derogatory sense of the word. Nevertheless the equipment should be expensive, and suggest a lightly worn technological know-how. One of those foreign gramophones that show their insides is a safe choice, and the hi-fi speakers should be small and inconspicuous, but extremely powerful.

YOUR COLLECTION

There are no absolute rules here, but several useful hints, most of them negative, should be borne in mind. As in record shops there are three basic categories: Classical, Jazz, and Pop, but unlike record shops there should be no suggestion that they are best separated. There are in our context only acceptable and unacceptable records, but for convenience, I shall deal with them separately.

(A) Classical

The thing here is to avoid *popular* classical music, especially of the "gems from" . . . or "three famous overtures" variety. It's all right to have a whole set of Beethoven's symphonies, or most of Wagner's "Ring," but for odd records obscurity is the rule. As a short cut, for those who have no knowledge of classical music, the sleeves provide a reliable guide. Avoid photographs of velvet curtains with violins resting in front of them on polished surfaces, beware reproductions of old masters, picturesque views of the Alps, busts of the composer, or neo-impressionist paintings of ballet dancers. Obscure architectural details may be all right, but to avoid mistakes go for plain covers in shades of vomit with rather heavy Germanic typography. You needn't play much classical music but it's not a bad wheeze to be discovered listening to some unaccompanied medieval plain song or a bit of the music from a baroque masque when people arrive. Don't take it off, turn it down reluctantly but graciously, and replace it by something more frivolous after it's finished.

(B) Jazz

Here it's all very much a question of the age of the collector, who, if over say thirty-five, may allow himself a certain amount of "chimes at midnight" sentimentality. Old LPs, even if ten-inch, that extinct category, are perfectly all right and so are re-issues of records which up until now were only available on 78s. The odd folk-blues, preferably recorded on a prison farm, a scratched Morton, an obscure 'twenties woman singer, are all acceptable. You can afford to be very insistent about the merits of Charlie Parker or Billie Holliday, especially when a bit drunk or high. Avant-garde jazz on the other hand should be represented, but is best avoided on the turntable, but it's quite OK to make use of it in place of the pre-party classical record as above. Certain periods are temporarily out of favour, "soul" for example, but don't throw them out. Stick them away next to the Christmas decorations. They'll be in again. Record sleeves in jazz are of no importance. They are all in the worst taste of their period.

(C) Pop

Pop is trickiest of all. A few old rock-and-roll LPs are fine, but as to what's new it's as well to recruit the services of a trendy adolescent. Be ruthless about pop. If you do play it, play it painfully loud. A mid-period Beatle record played at a volume over which people can still talk can do you irreparable damage.

Bits and Pieces

No plays or poems, and go easy on the thirty shillings and forty shillings camp. Film scores are a current problem, but if you *must* have them make sure they are on the American label, and get rid of them before the British premiere. In the 'fifties and very early 'sixties the same rule applied to the American musical but since "My Fair Lady" they have become unacceptable in any circumstance.

The final but extremely thorny category is what to do about "funny records". American again certainly, and preferably badly recorded in night-clubs with plenty of drunken laughter, but the comedian should be unknown in this country, and his every other joke should depend on an intimate knowledge of New York politics or Yiddish Broadway slang. Funny records of this kind serve a double function. They impress and bore, and can therefore be used to drive people home when you want to go to bed.

Old funny records, Tom Lehrer or "Noel Coward at Las Vegas" spell social death. Give them to your local Oxfam shop but for God's sake make sure nobody sees you taking them.

Glamour Guide

THE SERVICES

It is glamorous—

> To ride in triumph through Persepolis
> To be stoned by dervishes at Omdurman
> To charge the wrong guns and get killed
> To be brought home, like Nelson, in a barrel of rum
> To jump a horse over a billiard table in the mess
> To have served under Lord Mountbatten
> To go in on D-Day
> To be a submariner and sink an aircraft carrier with all hands
> To shoot down an aircraft from another aircraft
> To be a private with the VC
> To lose one eye, or one arm
> To have a nice young earl as one's aide-de-camp

It is not glamorous—

> To liberate Ostend in a mobile bath unit
> To be stoned by children in Londonderry
> To charge the right guns and get killed
> To be brought home from Vietnam sewn in a body bag
> To play leapfrog in the Methodist Canteen
> To have served under Lord Wigg
> To go in on D-Plus-One Day
> To be a sniper and blow men's brains out one by one
> To bring down an aircraft by anti-aircraft fire
> To be a brigadier with the MBE
> To lose two eyes, or two arms
> To have a quarter share in a slovenly batman

*"Why did you wake me up? I was
just having the most wonderful dream."*

"... and, my dear, jealous!"

CRIME

It is glamorous—

> To be arrested at a major airport for having cannabis worth £500,000
>
> To have a bunch of good-looking young women to help with one's murders
>
> To be written about by Peta Fordham or Tony Parker in a quality newspaper
>
> To stow away on a P & O liner
>
> To be escorted through London in a Black Maria with sirens screaming and headlights glaring
>
> To be an incompetent female hijacker of aircraft
>
> To be jailed for life in No. 1 Court, The Old Bailey, with all one's women screaming at the judge
>
> To break the windows of Barclays Bank
>
> To be a masked cat burglar at St. Tropez
>
> To be buried with a floral machine-gun on one's coffin

It is not glamorous—

> To be picked up for putting beer can rings in a parking meter
>
> To be a lone strangler
>
> To have one's memoirs ghosted in the *News of the World*
>
> To bilk British Railways
>
> To be marched in handcuffs across Liverpool Street Station
>
> To be a successful shoplifter
>
> To be put on probation at Leeds
>
> To break the windows of a betting shop
>
> To steal handbags at one's local Odeon
>
> To be disposed of quietly to an anatomy school

JOURNALISM

It is glamorous—

To write up novels in *Nova*

To tell the Prime Minister that now's the time to get rid of blockheads

To be Jilly Cooper in the *Sunday Times*

To go into action with the Red Devils

To be the only reporter on Everest

To be a motoring correspondent and thrash Lamborghinis round the Alps

To be Art Editor of *Playboy*

To be Editor of the Year

To be jailed for refusing to assist the State in its enquiries

To travel to Bangkok to photograph temples through the legs of fashion models

To take down the words of any film director

It is not glamorous—

To write up novels in *The Lady*

To tell women that now's the time to get rid of blackheads

To be Des Wilson in the *Observer*

To come out of a pub with the red devils

To be the only reporter on Everest with frostbite

To be a gardening editor and cover sweet pea shows at Wantage

To be Art Editor of *Health and Strength*

To be Free Dress Pattern Editor of the Year

To be sacked for refusing to assist Rupert Murdoch in his fantasies

To travel to Brighton to photogtaph the staff outing of Marks and Spencers

To take down donors' names from wreaths at the crematorium

"You sent for me, J.B.?"

"I can't remember it's name, but it leaves mature skin supple and fresh again, is as light as a Snowflake, rich with vitamins and moisturisers, items from a base of precious natural essences, contains exclusive bio-natural extracts, is a self-pampering treatment for tired and ageing skin, and is recommended for women whose quest for beauty knows no bounds."

Are Diamond's Still a Girl's Best Friend?

VIRGINIA IRONSIDE

THE editor of a newspaper I worked for, dredging the
bottom of the barrel for a story, once had the bright idea
of hiring a real diamond piece (in the shape of a hairpiece, for
heaven's sake) for which the young female staff would draw
straws. The idea was that the winner would write about her
experiences and try to convey the metamorphosis she under-
went and the reaction of her friends. Thank God I pulled a
long straw and the "lucky" winner was obliged to spend a
week with this glittering gem sparkling in her hair, attracting
undisguised mirth around the office and frank dismay among
her friends, whose reactions varied from "I'm not going to take
you to the Wimpy with that thing in yer barnet" to the
lecherous "I don't think we should go out alone with those
diamonds without a bodyguard. Maybe we should spend the
evening in at my place."

Far from turning into a magical international-setter
overnight she just felt a fool, and the weekend to remember
was only recalled as one of the most dull and humiliating of
her life. So much for diamonds.

Diamonds just don't mean that much these days, except in
terms of hard cash and once you're on to hard cash, then why
not just cut the crap and hand over the tenners?

That's not to say (in case any potential gift givers get the
wrong idea) that presents aren't always welcome. Personally
I'd never say no to half a crown and if a man wanted to lure
me to bed he could do worse than hold out a country cottage
as bait. A few shares would be welcome (but a premium bond,
so often described as "the chance to win £25,000" wouldn't);
even something dull like the lease on a profitable office block
in the city wouldn't be sniffed at. It's the things that can't be
converted into cash without being very conspicuous by their
absence that are to be avoided. A Picasso might be all very
nice, but if he's going to spot the pale patch on the wall when
you've carted it off to Christie's, then it's a non-starter.
Diamonds are much the same; you can't flog them without
their absence being noticed. It's the same with a mink coat or
a Rolls-Royce.

Not that I can talk. I've never been offered anything except
a free meal and a show. Someone once gave me a cardigan.
No one's ever offered me the starring part in his movie as a
reward for services rendered and much as I long to sleep my
way to the top, employers these days boringly seem to rely
more on talent than expertise in bed. It's a pretty sorry state

of affairs when a girl can't use her physical assets to get ahead, whether it's to get financially more secure or to fulfil ambition in her career.

Two things have put paid to the "diamonds are a girl's best friend" idea. One is that in an affluent society the few girls who still hold out are going to want a lot more than a measly old diamond to lure them into the clutches of a man. In fact the premium would be so high it'd be better to stick to the ageless winner, the modest bunch of violets or even the proposal of marriage.

The other thing is the permissive society. Chicken used to be a Sunday treat and now it's just a boring old Monday, Tuesday, Wednesday fill-in. Same with sex. There's just too much of it about to put it at a premium. So Nancy says no, she shan't unless she's given a diamond necklace, well, stuff Nancy because Sheila will do it for a steak and salad and come to think of it Pauline will do it for nothing. In fact, burrow a little further into the little black book and there's always Deborah who'll not only do it for nothing but give you a double whisky, a good breakfast and wash your shirts into the bargain.

And come to think of it, as a girl maybe it would be a good idea to get hold of a few diamonds. Not for yourself but to distribute to very special, but reluctant, men. "B-but, Virginia . . . they're . . . they're beautiful," he'll sob as he opens the box containing a pair of shimmering diamond cufflinks, before falling into your arms to let you wreak your will upon him. Diamonds may well become a *man's* best friend before long. Diamonds *and* dogs. Some people have all the luck.

Milliner. *"You can now see, Sir, how entirely the character of the little hat has changed when placed at what we call a 'saucy' angle."*

131

The Gift-For-The-Man-Who-Has-Everything Industry

A searching probe by GEORGE 'I-Who-have-Nothing' MIKES

DURING the Christmas season—which nowadays lasts from mid-August (when you have to post by sea-mail your parcels to New Zealand) to the end of March (by when you have made your last exchanges and have got rid of the last gift-tokens)—a grave, terrifying and tormenting problem rears its ugly head: *What to Give to the Person Who Has Everything?*

In the past, when words meant what they seemed to mean, this was an easy question to answer. *Nothing*, unless you wanted to duplicate his or her possessions. I know from the *Sunday Express* that gold-plated lavatory pulls, shaped like a Bunny-girl's legs, came on the market last year. So you could give MWHE (the Man Who Has Everything) a gold-plated lavatory-pull, shaped like a Bunny-girl's leg. This year, however, the same harrowing problem faces you once again, unless, of course, MWHE wants *two* gold-plated lavatory pulls, shaped like a *pair* of a Bunny-girl's legs, which would seem proper and reasonable to me.

As no family can possibly have all the worries under the sun, this *What to Give a Person Who Has Everything* is not one of our acute agonies of the day or the season. In our household the Lady of the House has never accepted a sable coat from me with a yawn and the wounding remark: "Good God, a sable again?!" She has never made a vulgar scene because I gave her yet another diamond ring or emerald-studded ruby brooch. She has never thrown a platinum platter at me, with contemptuous disdain. I, myself, am the veritable prototype of MWHN—the Man Who Has Nothing. I have travelled all over the world on several occasions but never bought any souvenirs anywhere—no ceremonial, harikari sword in Kyoto, no Japanese transistor in Fiji, no tartan tie in Inverness. We do not have one single golden lavatory chain between ourselves. I am shaving with a safety razor about twelve or thirteen years old which is more ridiculously out-of-date than wearing green silk breeches with white stockings or being courteous to elderly people. True, in the last seven years the thought has flashed through my mind every morning that I ought to buy a new razor. But a few minutes later I think of other matters. Often—most unselfishly—of the problems of others, for example, *What to Give to the Person Who Has Everything?*

Going through the advertisements and catalogues it is hard—and I presume utterly pointless—to remember that

Christmas celebrates the birth of a poor man and not of an MWHE. A man who never had a Christmas-present (which, in his case, would have been a birthday-present) in all his short life. But times have changed. I know a little boy who actually believes that Christmas commemorates the birth of Mr. Selfridge. Or Mr. Harrod—he isn't sure.

Be that as it may, I began to wonder, what would I really fancy if I were a MWHE. Would I appreciate for instance—warmly recommended by one of our best department stores—a superb dining-room suite from Spain, with ivory painted finish, marble-topped table, complete with tapestry seats—costing £1400. I am not sure I would. I would appreciate, of course, the thought but I do have a dining-room suite (admittedly, the table has no marble top, on the chairs no sign of Spanish tapestry and not an ounce of ivory in the whole outfit) but the arrival of nine huge pieces of furniture might cause some embarrassment. Or would I like a clock which needs no winding at all and is framed in delicately chased brass? Unfair, I think. For a lot of MWHE winding their clocks and watches are the only physical exercise they get and these gifts tend to deprive them even of that. Or would I care to get—or rather to give—the "smallest watch in the world," hardly visible to the naked eye but generously studded with platinum and diamonds and costing no more than £3550? Or a kangaroo? Or a baby elephant? Or a paper-weight, starting from £75?

No, I do not want all these. They are simple devices to get rid of large sums of money and I should appreciate something into which a little thought has gone. The greatest innovation, for instance, struck me as a very lucky idea: a portable radio covered with mink. Few of us feel the actual *need* for a mink-covered radio, however forbidding the weather-forecast may sound, but it would be hard to deny that only a very special brain could have thought that one out.

Then I suddenly saw the system in it. It is not so difficult, after all. These chaps and girls who keep the MWHE constantly in mind, follow a few definite patterns.

1. *Combine the incongruous.* Cover your radio with mink. Gild your lavatory pull. Place tiny electric windscreen-wipers on peoples' spectacles, with batteries in their pockets. Use Persian carpets for towels. Disguise peoples' telephones so that they look like books, bottles or renaissance jewel-boxes. And disguise their books, bottles and renaissance jewel-boxes to look like telephones.

2. *Make people buy utterly strange things.* Persuade men to wear tights instead of socks. (Tights for men are terrific sellers this year.) Tell them to use perfume. Not just after-shave lotions and deodorants but perfume which costs real money. Sell Bibles to babies; weight-lifting equipment to the over-eighty; encyclopaedias to the illiterate (a booming trade, actually); bras to men; teach women to shave.

3. *Produce double-purpose things.* But be careful that the

133

two purposes should have nothing really to do with each other. There is not much point in manufacturing an adding-up machine which can also subtract, because that much is only expected. The armchair which can be transformed into a bed is a sensible, practical idea—so useless for this purpose. I see a new, rather long desk-lighter which can also be used as a foot-rule. The MWHE may have—indeed, must have—a lighter; he also must have a ruler and a measure. But he cannot have a lighter with which he can measure the length of strings or a ruler with which he can light his cigar. And to do that must give him tremendous satisfaction; a sense of power, I daresay. You can play your gramophone records on electric toasters. (The Man Who Doesn't Have Everything must remain satisfied to play *his* on a stereo.) You can use your alarm-clock as a tape-recorder and one of our department stores plans to bring out for next Christmas a cat which barks at strangers at night.

4. *The Personal Touch.* This seems to be one of the most important features for the truly discriminating. All this mass-produced rubbish must have a truly personal touch. You may have, for example, your monogram—your initials—on ice-cubes. I often dream of it, how happy and delighted I would be, if I could drop into my gin and tonic a piece of ice with a "G" on it. On the other hand, would not that be a trifle humiliating for guests of mine, called Michael, or Reginald? Or take "Your Initial Tie." Although initials on ties are as old as humanity itself, well, say as ties themselves, nevertheless, this is advertised as a "first edition" of one of our famous stores. The reason for this is that the design was specially created for them in Italy and it "transforms the initial into a subtle, modern repeat-pattern." Can you get any more personal than that? Yes, you can. A few letters—O, Q, U, X, Y and Z—are not available. The Italian artist is as incorruptible as that. He had no inspiration to design ties with an O—so Oscar, Oswald, Orson and Otto may have a radio with mink but cannot have a personal tie. And what about the others? As if it were not hard enough to be called Quentin, Uchtred, Yorick and Zachariah, they—on top of it all—are deprived of their personal ties.

But perhaps all this is on the wrong track, anyway. I know a few MWHE and I feel that most of them would appreciate a good book by a decent writer. Not that they would read it—far from it—but that's the one single commodity most of them do not possess. Or what about giving to the MWHE a little personal thought, a few words truly your own, an idea or two which *you* have thought out and not a designer in Italy or a specialist who carves your highly personalized and very subtle initials in ice cubes? But, on second thoughts, there is no getting away from it. As soon as the need for such things is established, Human Kindness will be mass-produced in tins, with your initials on top, and Personal Thought will come in beautiful Christmas boxes, covered with mink.

Kind-Hearted Niece. *"Well, Uncle, I call him shockingly over-dressed. Your little pendant is* **much** *smarter."*

It's Not what You've Got, It's the Way that You Spend It

LORD MANCROFT on style

THE Prodigal Son, as you may remember, wasted his substance with riotous living, but whether or not he did this in style is uncertain. No tales have come down to us of rejoicing with the daughters of the Philistines in Gath, nor (perish the thought) has anything been published about triumphing with the daughters of the uncircumcised in the streets of Askelon. Nevertheless, the Prodigal Son had to fall back on pig swill for luncheon, which must have been very embarrassing for a nice Jewish boy like him.

I myself have mixed feelings about money. It doesn't, of course, buy friends, though it does allow you a better class of enemy, and there are few sorrows, however poignant, in which a good income can be of no avail. Money is the sixth sense that helps you to enjoy the other five. It would therefore be nice if Providence could think less about money itself, and more about the sort of people to whom it is given. Any fool can make money, but spending it in style is more difficult. In the cash box the dividing line between style and banality is finely drawn.

Diamond Jim Brady used to light his cigar with a dollar bill, and this is very bad style indeed. It's vulgar and pointless, and the smell of burning dollar bills would probably ruin even an American cigar. But Diamond Jim redressed the balance when he sent Lilian Russell three dozen roses each containing a diamond in place of the customary dew-drop. That, I think, was charming, and it stops just short of ostentation. Four dozen would have spoilt the whole thing, as sheer size so often does.

For instance, you've really got to have the taste of a Sun King to inject style into anything like as grandiose as Versailles. And for this reason I'm reserving judgment on the Cheops boys and their pyramids, and on Solomon in all his rather brazen glory. I am, however, glad that Solomon had the wisdom not to marry that flashy Queen of Sheba. Nobody has to work so hard for his money as the man who's married it, and this brings us naturally to Mr. Richard Burton who has both married it and made it. I don't think Miss Elizabeth Taylor has ever appeared as the Queen of Sheba so what I would like to see would be Cleopatra in "The Life of Elizabeth Taylor."

Granny Taylor like Mrs. Jackie Onassis seems to be a classically compulsive spender, not really of style so much as sheer bravura. Wouldn't it be nice therefore to let them loose together in Bond Street, locking their husbands up in Marks and Spencer, which would probably be taken over before teatime.

Pugnacious spending can be bad for style. You mustn't buy Renoirs just to trump your neighbour's Cézannes. And don't let your wife go alone to Yves St. Laurent's place in Paris. Women can seldom buy clothes in style when they are alone, because they seldom dress to please either men or themselves. They dress to annoy other women.

Revengeful spending, however, can have style. Lord Nuffield once wanted to join a certain golf club, but some of the members objected. So he bought the whole club, and only elected the members who had smiled upon him. I think that's nice.

There can, of course, be as much style in the reasons for spending money as there is in the spending itself. I remember once sitting next to Bud Flanagan at a charity auction, and I praised the generosity of those who were pushing up the bids. "Nonsense," Bud snorted, "Conscience Money. None of them has put in a proper tax return for years."

I hope the same principle doesn't apply to those who spend money on building new libraries, or endowing Chairs of Chiropody. Unkind people suggest that this may also be done to ensure that the Princess will actually come to their daughter's dance, or that they may eventually trump their neighbour's Knighthood with a Peerage. I'm sure this can't be so! That's no better than giving the head-waiter a fat tip as you come into the restaurant in order to guarantee service to come. That's a bribe rather than a tip, and it's the negation of spending in style.

Flapper. *"I say, Smithers, have you got an alarum clock?"*
Butler. *"I have, Miss Joan."*
Flapper. *"Well, just bring it here and set it to cocktail time, will you?"*

Mark you, tipping can be a test for any stylist. You needn't be a millionaire to do it well, but you've got to have panache. I recall with affection the standards set by my friend, Charlie Cringleford, who was up at The House with me in the 'thirties. He was by no account a rich man, but he was a very pretty spender all the same. When he was in the Army he used to send his shirts home every week from India to be washed. And his soldier servant once found a note on the dresser saying, "Please put two bottles of the Cockburn '12 by my bedside and call me the day after tomorrow."

When he was at Oxford Charlie had been the proud owner of a 1923 bull-nosed Morris-Cowley. Despite the Dean's disapproval, it was called God, because it moved in a mysterious way. Everything about the car made a noise except the horn; it did about two telegraph poles to the gallon with the wind behind it, and it was painted red down one side and blue down the other, to confuse the witnesses in the event of an accident.

Well, one evening Charlie was bidden to a smart rout at Londonderry House. He drove up to the front door in this bizarre vehicle, resplendent in top hat, white tie and tails. "Shall I park it for you, M'lord?" asked the linkman. "No, no," said Charlie loftily, "keep it for yourself, my good man. By all means, keep it," and he strolled through the front door peeling off his white kid gloves.

At this point I should declare my own preference. I am not interested in cars, or chiropody, and, although I shall have my ears boxed for saying so, I think Renoir is an overrated artist.

On the other hand I greatly admire Sir Joseph Camps, who may possibly not be known to you. He it was who refused to accompany Captain Cook on his trip to Australia unless he was allowed to take with him not one but two horn players to entertain him during dinner. There's richness for you! But when my football pools come home I shall blue the proceeds not just on two horns but on a whole private orchestra.

Of course I realise there's nothing very original about this. Nebuchadnezzar did it with his cornet, flute, harp, sackbut, psaltery, dulcimer, and all the other kinds of music to be found in Daniel 3. v. 5, and a pretty cacophonous combo that must have been. I have mixed feelings, too, about the Emperor Meiji whose Court musician once composed a Concerto for twenty-four Japanese singing-mice and a bass trombone. Unfortunately, at the first run through the trombone inhaled an alto singing-mouse, and the whole project had to be abandoned. Nevertheless, the basic idea was sound.

The German princelings of the eighteenth century were no great shakes as rulers, but Bach, Handel and Haydn started on their way to fame and Paradise with the Grand Duke or the Elector's little drawing-room band. My band will be private, but far from little, and whether the players like it or not I shall conduct it myself. I was once allowed to conduct the

Bonn University Student Orchestra, and a maggotty-headed lot of layabouts they were. Would you believe it, by the time I'd got as far as bar 200 in the last movement of Beethoven's 7th they'd got no further than bar 182? I had to bring them up pretty sharply on no less than three occasions, but on the third the leader said that if I did it again they'd play exactly as I was conducting.

I realise, of course, that a private orchestra costs the earth. Indeed, if you have to ask how much, you obviously can't afford one. Like a yacht. And, talking of yachts, did any Prime Minister ever disport himself in greater style than Mr. Heath in Morning Glory II? It's all very well for Mr. H. Wilson to grumble, but let's wait and see how he spends the proceeds of his Memoirs. Dr. Johnson spent the money he earned from the first number of The Rambler on oysters for his cat Hodge. If Mr. Wilson can show greater style than that I'll eat my hat. Even if I have to buy a new one specially for the job, I'll eat it—and in style.

"Now, that looks a nice place."

6.30 to 8.0

You may as well learn to know what you are in for. This type of host will give you sherry, a goodish Amontillado, but without the option. It is unthinkable that anything less genteel should be offered in his house. If in doubt, study your hostess.

This is a sherry house, too. But note your host's moustache. He is more sure of himself, more a man of the world. After the opening "This is a tolerable sherry, I think you'll find," he is quite likely to add "Or a whisky-and-soda, if you prefer it?" That, however, is the end of it. Only the thick-skinned, unembarrassed by background consultations and long delays, should press for whisky and *water*.

Of course if there are waiters with trays, the immediate choice is between dry martini and a pretty medium sherry—perhaps an Amoroso. Take one. Take either. It is a kind of admission ticket, something to hold in the hand while searching about to see whether the caterers have set up a bar with a white cloth on it in some distant corner. There may be gin-and-tonics over there.

140

Oh, dear! This means you are going to get a "Ferguson Special" (if Ferguson is the man's name), poured liberally and repeatedly from ready-mixed jugs. The dangerous alcoholic qualities of this drink are laughingly denied by your host before anyone has thought of suggesting them. It consists almost entirely of orange squash.

Stand by to agree that it is *so* much more interesting to have an occasional change from the eternal gins and sherries—"or so my sister and I think." What is it? Portuguese rosé, very likely.

Be careful here. This rosy-faced busybody isn't your host. He's that friend who is "always glad to lend a hand," and doesn't give a damn what he mixes with what. After all, it's not his vodka.

Champagne cocktails for a certainty, even before you have a chance to spot the shape of the glasses. It's hard to say exactly why, unless it's something about the way the guests are standing—as if the men were in pink coats, you know. Everybody knows everybody here, you will find. With one exception.

This man's manners are appalling. You'd think he could interrupt his conversation with that woman to say something more warm and welcoming than "You'll find everything over there." The consolation is that you will.

A Load of Old Flannel

JOHN TAYLOR opens his Weekend Wardrobe

FORTY years back the uniform of the working man on holi-day consisted of his best blue serge suit, a tennis shirt with the top turned neatly down on the collar of the jacket, and a pair of white plimsolls.

The plimsolls and the open-necked shirt were clear con-cessions to comfort; but the blue serge suit was a confusing facet of holiday gear. It evolved from the fact that in those days not-working was connotated with the Sabbath—and on the Sabbath you wore your best blue serge suit to please God. The rest of the week was spent in overalls or "working clothes"—garments which were hardly suitable for social occasions or the passing fancies of leisure. Without the extensive wardrobe enjoyed by the working classes today, the only alternative to working clothes was your "best." On holiday, therefore, you wore your blue serge suit.

Weekend clothes at any level other than the relatively prosperous are pretty new; but then so is the weekend. When everybody worked long hours every day including Saturday, and spent large periods of Sunday at church, leisure clothes had no need to be invented. The middle classes and the upper classes might experiment with such decadent sartorial experiments as the lounge suit, or the short morning coat, but the large mass of the populace had only clothes to work in and clothes to go to church in. The steady diminution of the working week has changed the situation.

For the average man now has more time to himself than he is prepared to surrender to God or his employer. A forty-hour work-week allows about fifty hours for sleep and something like close on eighty hours to please yourself. The weekend spreads now from the post-prandial lethargy of Friday lunchtime to the glum resurrection of ten o'clock on Monday morning. And as if that wasn't long enough, there is the creeping familiarity of something longer called a "long" weekend—from Thursday to Tuesday. The economic considerations in buying clothes is suddenly transferred from work to leisure—for one naturally selects clothing in terms of the greatest wear period. The whole country is tending to dress for the weekend for the whole of the week.

Even so recently as before World War Two, sports coats and flannel trousers could only be worn to the office on Saturday morning. It was regarded as a pretty corrupting concession at the time and is difficult to remember nowadays—when in any case nobody still works on a Saturday morning. But sports coats and flannels did not disappear because Saturday working disappeared. The relaxed clothes are simply stealthily applied to the rest of the week.

It is possible that from this steady decline in sartorial rectitude has evolved the fact that we are today a nation of layabouts. For comfort induces relaxation. Put a man in a bed and he will probably soon fall asleep. Put him in leisure clothes and he will act in a leisured manner. Urgency will desert him and his work will suffer. The national economy is ruined for the want of waistcoats and hard collars. Discipline has a variety of manifestations and the lack of it a variety of effects.

The term "sports" coat was in itself a misnomer, of course. You couldn't have played any active game in it, and there was no particular functionalism in grey flannel trousers in an era which had already accepted short trousers for any really active pursuit. But one knows that tennis players wore long white trousers until the start of the Second World War, and that the football trousers of the nineteen-forties were not much shorter.

The weekend has always been the period for sporting life, and it is because of this that the functional properties of sporting clothes have impinged themselves more and more on ordinary weekend daywear. Mobility, too, has been a basic essential of the weekend—and thus we find in all our clothes an increasing influence of the motor car and the crystallised influences of the horse.

In general, too, the evolution ahead seems to suggest something in similar terms to beach wear; and here again, time off is the basic consideration.

The arrival of short trousers for every-day wear is inevitable now that shorts are regarded as perfectly acceptable at the weekend. The mini-skirt is the skating skirt of the nineteen-thirties and the tennis dress of the nineteen-forties. Bare midriff (bikini) dresses are widely worn for evening already and several were around the town during the recent heat wave. The topless is okayed on some beaches already, and will doubtless make its dancing way into the City before another generation is out.

For the fashions are now being set by the younger people and not by the crusty old Establishment—and the younger generation is entirely weekend orientated.

When the topless fashion was tried a few years ago it failed because it was up against people sired and dammed by Victorians. Next time round its opposition will not be nearly so implacable. In Chicago, at the time, a Miss Shelley pioneered the topless on the shore of Lake Michigan and was immediately remanded in custody whilst a legal wrangle evolved around the testaments of witnesses claiming they had once seen Shelley plain. But it is significant that much of the criticism was not levelled at an aesthetic level but at a concern with her *right* to dress as she pleased. Toleration was already paving the way for another attempt later. The widening acceptance of see-through fashions is the result.

Ever ready for the relaxing results of the fad at the time, the 57-strong chain of Mecca dance halls in 1964 prepared for the

Saturday-night dancing crowd by issuing an edict to the effect that ladies in topless ballgowns would be refused entrance unless they adjusted their dress before arriving. They even announced that a selection of "Bosom Covers" would be available at the doors of all Mecca establishments for such pioneering spirits as had braved the journey thereto.

Their anxiety seemed a little exaggerated. Dangers of inflaming a social contact into a follow-up of Saturday night deep into Sunday morning would be slight during the gyrations of a normal ballroom sequence. The close juxtaposition of the partners should serve to hide the front of the female partner from general view in all but the more modern or the more old-fashioned dances. There could be no visual impropriety at all in the close-locked embrace of a night club shuffle—and even in the wilder convolutions of a shake or twist about the most damage the male partner would sustain would be a smashed *boutonnière*. If the influence of weekend clothes continues, the trend to nakedness would seem inevitable.

It might be only just in time if we are to suffer the horrifying effects of another style of clothing which seems mainly manifested at the weekend—either in any relaxed circle of under thirty-year-olds or in those dreary "marches" which seem planned for every weekend nowadays.

Tight jean trousers, the badge of all weekending teenagers, offers deeper stress than simply the sharp attack of haemorrhoids induced by sitting down protestingly on a cold wet street. During the stint of Duncan Sandys as Minister of Defence a few years ago, he had replied to a question in the House concerning the dangers of atomic fallout by referring to a report issued by Swedish scientists engaged on mutation research. Opined the Swedes: "The unnatural heat caused by the wearing of tight trousers is likely to have a cumulatively harmful effect upon the male organs." They suggested the kilt as a sensible alternative, forwarding their belief that tight trousers could cause 1,000 times more genetic harm than could radiation—and that people habitually clad in such clothing would have a spontaneous mutation rate eighty-five per cent higher than nudists.

An American physicist named Edward Teller also suggested there might be more danger to future generations through too-warm clothing than from fallout, and a BMA journal named Family Doctor connected certain cases of sterility with a fondness for too-warm baths.

How clear that possibility is is moot. But certain it is that the whole trend in what we wear is towards lighter and lighter and less and less. The increasing emptiness of life will be reflected in an increasing emptiness in the wardrobe, and as the steadily growing weekend develops into something like the end of the week, there will be no need for clothes at all as we sit in a jelly of atrophied muscle and uncommunicative blob. Have a nice weekend.

High Bills in Jamaica

E. S. TURNER on the Caribbean gold rush

IT looks like a ghastly misprint, but it isn't. The daily rate per person in a cottage at Frenchman's Cove, Jamaica, during the winter, is £75.

You wouldn't mind paying a little more? Well, there's the Fontainebleau Hotel at Miami Beach where, as Alan Whicker has revealed, they will relieve you of £200 a day, if you insist on a suite. You can also pay prodigally to be seasick in a cruise liner (but transportation is thrown in).

What do you get for that sort of money, apart from sun, in a winter playground? You hope to get what Brooklands motor-racing track used to offer: *The right crowd and no crowding.* You also enjoy the spiritual satisfaction of drinking rum punches on a hot white beach while your friends back home are screwing up their eyes against the sleet (some of them may be ski-ing in the Alps, but what is St. Moritz compared to Montego Bay?).

You may be one who worries about social contrasts, but in your cottage colony in Jamaica you are shielded from sight of shanties and the great billboards which proclaim YOU DON'T HAVE TO GET PREGNANT. That message is not directed to tourists. In any event, the American wives around you are mostly beyond impregnation.

To get a picture of a Caribbean winter playground, try this mental exercise. Suppose that all the best hotels on the Isle of Wight have been taken over by blacks for the benefit of wealthy black tourists. Assume that they have all the best coves and the best golf courses. Now assume that the only well-paid jobs for white people in these resorts are those of taxi-driver, waiter, chambermaid and beach boy, with perhaps an occasional assistant managership of an hotel. Finally, assume that the luckless remainder of the white population are being urged not to get pregnant.

An improbable situation? But that's how it is, with the colours reversed, on the North Coast of Jamaica. The taxi-drivers and waiters do not want to change it (in Montego Bay somebody pointed out to me a waiter with six cars for hire). But the less fortunate inhabitants see tourists only as creatures from outer space; creatures who, from time to time, emerge from their enclaves, clownishly dressed, in fun buggies, possibly to buy a few native wares or possibly (since Jamaica has free port status) to order a Wedgwood dinner service or a set of Swedish glasses.

It will never be easy for a holidaying tycoon to integrate with peasants. But if a visitor feels guilty at not meeting the "natives" he can always consult the Jamaica Tourist Board's list of "Interesting People" who are willing to talk to tourists. They include a Colonel of Maroons, who dwells in

Accompong, in the wild Cockpit Country, where the British Army fought its grim Maroon Wars. The Colonel's hobby is meeting tourists; other hobbies of the Interesting People are orchids, real estate, stenography, reporting and family planning.

The North Coast of Jamaica is a never-never land haunted by ghosts of the larger-than-life: Churchill and Nelson; Columbus and Errol Flynn; Beaverbrook and Ivor Novello; Ian Fleming and Noel Coward; not forgetting those absentee slave-owners, the eccentric William Beckford of Fonthill and Edward Moulton-Barrett, the tyrant of Wimpole Street.

The most talked-about and least substantial ghost is now being exploited by a property millionaire. It is that of Annie Palmer, the '"White Witch" of Rose Hall, supposedly a Voodoo-crazed slave-flogger who poisoned one husband, stabbed a second, strangled a third and was then strangled by a slave. Her great house was until recently a spectral ruin, but it has been restored to its mahogany-and-four-poster splendours by John Rollins, one-time Lieutenant-Governor of Delaware, as centrepiece of a big resort development. Although the tale of Annie is resounding nonsense, inspired by a popular novel, Rollins has seized upon it gratefully; and it may be that Jamaica needs the legend of a wicked plantocrat as much as he does.

Like the ineffable Fred Pontin, who says he is willing to build up the entire Mediterranean coastline if there is a demand for it, the developers would be happy to leave the North Coast of Jamaica without a strip of public beach. However, the Government insists on a reasonable quorum of open beaches, in between Holiday Inns and Playboy Hotels and cottage colonies.

"It's a tough area to crack so we concentrate all our best men at that branch once a year."

The redoubtable Frenchman's Cove, the creation of Garfield Weston, differs from other colonies in that its cottages are fashioned from best Jamaican limestone and enjoy rather more privacy, more cosily romantic views and more elegant landscaping. Besides cottages, it has a "great house" (Jamaica is a great place for great houses). Each cottage has its own maid and—that extra touch—its own butler, to whom one is encouraged to dictate wild culinary fancies, in the hope that they can be realised. Each cottage also has its own powered golf cart for transport. A helicopter used to be available on demand, for fishing or sightseeing, but I was chagrined to find that it had been withdrawn. "Within reason" global telephone calls are still free. Although tips are discouraged, the Americans keep on giving them, though possibly not at the rate of fifteen per cent on £700 a week (the winter rate for two).

To social climbers, Frenchman's Cove poses the same challenge as Everest to mountain climbers. George Mikes has made the excellent suggestion that persons who have stayed there should be allowed to put FC after their names. The novelist V. S. Naipaul, who was invited to stay for a night, has left a moving account of the difficulties he had in trying to think of adequate luxuries for the butler to bring him.

At Frenchman's Cove the rates are slashed to £245 a week in summer, which is still high enough to stop the place being flooded with American secretaries (a fate which notoriously befalls the Bahamas in summer). It is not wholly tenanted by juiceless vice-presidents, however. They pointed out to me a cottage which had been occupied by an eminent jazz drummer, with family and entourage; his bill for six weeks was $30,000.

Prices like these encouraged the unscrupulous Portuguese tourist industry to point out that you can spend a fortnight's holiday on the Algarve for the price of a night in the Caribbean. To which the Caribbean retorts, Ah, but can you guarantee winter sun and a warm sea? To be fair, there are popular-priced playgrounds, even on the North Coast of Jamaica, where British package tour operators are already staking a claim. There may not be a Harmsworth or a Thyssen in the next hut and you may not have golden fluttering torches lighting the path to your door; yet you may still lie, rum punch in hand, beside the palms and watch for the elusive green flash which follows a Caribbean sunset.

But perhaps your idea of a winter playground is a rip-roaring metropolis rising in Miami style from the sea? A free port with an international shopping centre, restaurants of all nations and a casino? Well, there's Freeport-Lucaya on Grand Bahama. It wasn't there fifteen years ago and some wish it wasn't there now. But it's a grand place to buy Wedgwood ware and Swedish glass—if you're an American, that is: those free ports which stud the Caribbean are not really much help to the British. The Bahamas can furnish plenty of quiet idyllic spots in the Out Islands; and Britain enjoys her tiny triumph in that, even on remote cays, traffic (if any) must drive on the left.

"He's dictating postcards."

In the Bahamas they like you to buy your own winter playground, or at least a flat in a high white condominium. Or why not buy a whole island? On Bay Street, Nassau girl touts offer free flights to the development of your choice.

For my taste, some of the finest winter playgrounds are in the Windward and Leeward Islands. You can fly non-stop from Heathrow to Antigua and practise limbo dancing (squeezing under a horizontal pole) the same evening. I have visited a score of delectable hotels in the Antilles, not the least attractive being those which were carved from the jungle on the edge of the rain forest in Dominica. *Playgrounds?* On the edge of the rain forest? Naturally, you must devise your own games. For livelier delights, try St. Lucia, St. Vincent, Grenada . . . not to mention the French drive-on-the-right isles of Guadeloupe and Martinique.

Basically, these Antillean playgrounds resemble those of Jamaica, in that the tourists enjoy the best coves and golf courses. The hotels are frequently pioneered by American, Canadian and British couples and to say that they sometimes have staff problems is to put it mildly. But thanks to those Hotel Incentive Acts on the Jamaican model, there are ten-year tax concessions and the lucky hotelier can clean up while the fashion lasts.

John Osborne's play *West of Suez* is set on a Caribbean island where expatriates are trying to recreate a corner of England. You find these elderly dreamers in their newly erected bungalows everywhere from the Antilles to the Bahamas. They were tempted by sun, solitude, servants . . . but many of them looked bored. Perhaps they made the mistake of the man who, having found a brand of beer which suited him, decided to go to work in the brewery.

Azure seas, gentle breeze, distant lands, golden sands, heavenly views, cheap booze, are mostly between the lines in BASIL BOOTHROYD'S

Cruising Alphabet

AIR Conditioning is something cruise lines wish hadn't been invented. What with complaints either that it isn't working, or that coming in off the gale-swept sun deck into the shelter of the public rooms is like trying to find comfort in a butcher's refrigerator, they'd like to leave the customers to sweat and lump it: especially those who keep prodding the cabin installation with smuggled cutlery and setting off the sprinkler-valves by mistake. But it looks great in the advertising.

BOAT Drill. Don't turn up for it. No one will miss you, and if this is alarming it isn't half as bad as seeing big men ploughing through the women and children in a frenzy of self-preservation—and this only an exercise, in peril-free conditions, anyway.

CAPTAINS are notable for their Tables, which tend to accrete eminent drainage authorities, the Lady Mary Stiggins, and you if you don't watch it; also for their professional pigheadedness, which makes them sail, bang on time, in weather that would have kept Francis Drake tied up at the Hoe with extra hawsers.

DURATION should be as long as you can afford. Eight Dalmatian resorts in a four-day whiz means an unbroken roar of anchor-chains, followed by a year's marital debates on whether it was Split or Dubrovnik where you saw the eleventh century fresco with Ron Smith, Leeds, scratched across it.

"**E**NTIRELY Reconverted" is a bit of brochure talk designed to suggest trendy decor, reassuring radar equipment and top-grade seaworthiness, but it can also mean that when you open your cabin wardrobe you find it's mostly occupied by a big raw girder, giving you the unreasonable but persistent feeling that you're personally holding the whole ship together.

FLYING may be the way you have to reach the port of departure, and it's as well to check. If you're sweeping the Aegean with Epirotiki Lines, for instance—and there's nothing like Greek sailors for relaxing you in Greek waters, whereas you feel the Yugoslavs could collide with Naxos any time—it's no good hanging around Southampton expecting the *Orpheus* to sidle up. You'll find her at Piraeus: unless you forget, when directing the cab at Athens airport, that Orpheus and Piraeus both rhyme with revs.

GROOVY is what few ships' bands can be dubbed, but they make up by using enough amplifying equipment to put the generators on the blink, and even "Tea for Two" can crack a glass at twenty paces.

HORSE, Wooden. Just a mention, for the souvenir-crazy, that the trinket-stalls outside Troy are selling pieces of this. Or they were last year. It could all have gone by now.

"IMMEDIATE" is traditionally used in the daily programme of events to describe disembarkation for shore excursions, causing the deck to be packed from rail to rail, half an hour before the gangplank goes down, with a fighting mass of passengers tangled up in each other's light-meter straps and terrified of being left behind. As it's an hour after that before they're all off, bar the dead and wounded, you, who wisely aren't going, have an early choice of empty chairs. One of the finest cruise experiences is to spread out at leisure and watch the herds on the quay being sheep-dogged into their buses by the barking guides, or see the dutiful, dwindling crocodile as it disappears Hamelin fashion into the Old City of Rhodes, or toils, at the end of your binoculars, up the punishing pumice of Santorini.

"JUST Darling". The unvarying verdict of American ladies on all shore excursions. Also on the Captain, the squeakers issued free on Gala Night, the freighter unloading cement at the berth, and indeed everything. Americans should get a good PRO to kill their image as fussy travellers.

KORCULA. One of the chief places where no one can remember what happened there when they get home.

LIBRARY. Though universally well spoken of in the cruise literature, ships' libraries aren't wholly to be relied on, partly because of eccentric opening hours, partly because there's often nothing to open but a locked metal bar across a glass-fronted shelf containing five paperbacks. In German.

"MULTI-LINGUAL". A courtesy adjective used of the crew, meaning that when you ask for an extra pillow they say, "Sure, OK," take away your drinking-water carafe and don't come back. This is your own fault for not speaking Croat or Albanian. And are stewards on QE 2 cruises, it's worth wondering, any more helpful at getting extra pillows for Turks? Roll on Esperanto.

NAVARONE, The Guns of. This film, thanks to the sensibilities of the organisers, doesn't get many showings in ships' cinemas in the Aegean. The scene where a tempest rips up out of nowhere, reduces the ship to barrel staves and damned nearly drowns David Niven, could put thoughts into nervous heads. Bob Hope's early vehicles are more favoured, though cruise-goers of long standing avoid even those. It isn't only that it seems wrong for Hope to be up there clowning when their seats are side-slipping down a juddering trough: they just can't take "My Favourite Blonde" again.

OCTOBER. Go before then because of the weather (see above). You can miss a lot of meals you've paid for in advance.

PHOTOGRAPHY is the cruiser's curse. For real enjoyment leave all cameras at home, and see Naples through your actual wide-angle human eye, instead of a little smeary viewfinder. Picture-postcards do a better job anyway, and if your friends won't believe you've been there unless you're grinning in the foreground with your shirt done up on the wrong buttons, change your friends.

QUEUES. These are mainly at the Purser's office, and he usually stays in his room at the back until they've gone. This doesn't apply on the last night out, when you have to keep queuing if you want to pay your bar chits. Not that you do want to, but if you don't they won't let you have your passport back. Clever.

ROMANCE, holiday. Girls, remember that a tanned, sinewy officer gets upwards of six thousand melting looks per season; boys, that cute cruise hostesses are apt to be married to a tanned, sinewy officer on the sister-ship that keeps tying up alongside.

SUBMARINES. A spell of service in these is ideal for adapting to average cruise cabin dimensions.

TURN-ROUND begins as soon as journey's end is sighted. You are then obsolete as a passenger. You've had your fun. Go. (Provided tipping has been executed.)

UMBRELLAS, sun. It isn't surprising, perhaps, that there's always one socket without one in. What's surprising is that it's always by the one empty chair you thought you were so smart to spot. Calomine lotion is a good substitute.

V-FORM. Looking back on it all, the places you saw, the fun you had, what really lingers as sheer enjoyment is the smart way the organisers somehow managed to scrub *round* this.

WAKE, ship's obsession with movies of. See *Photography*, but if you've been fool enough to bring the cine, make a resolution to keep out of the stern. You've got enough wake footage from last year to last Robin Knox-Johnston a lifetime. Or do you think this one's different?

XENIA. Name of Greek hotels on practically all the Islands. They don't get you around like ships, but they're lovely and still. Planning for next year yet?

YARDARM. No licensing laws, and not even the need to wait for the sun to be over this before breaking out with the duty-free Tom Collins? You could come back an alcoholic. Don't worry. Though ships' bars are plentiful, and look open all the time, they're only open if the man behind them is a barman, and not some other indistinguishable white-coat on mere swabbing and pistachio-sorting. No English, but a master of the mime that sends you to the bar on another deck, which mimes you back to where you came from. Cuts the liquor costs, tones the system with lots of exercise, but doesn't mean that everyone else you see hasn't managed to get a drink somewhere. A mystery of the sea.

ZURICH, Gnomes of. Only to say that if Roy Jenkins is continuing the fifty quid limit to keep them happy, as it's widely bruited, they must be pretty miserable, the way we British tourists manage to line up at the ship's shop and clean it out of crocodile handbags and tape-recorders the moment we're out of the three-mile limit.

Lady. *"Tell me doctor—I want my husband to take me to Cannes. What ailment do you recommend?"*

The Best Car In The World

ALAN COREN

IF there is one fantasy laid down in childhood that sticks like a barnacle to the psyche, informing all we are and do for the next three score and ten, it is the metamorphosis dream; whereby at the drop of a magic word, the shambling agglomeration of inadequacies and insecurities that make up the average biped are suddenly shogged off, and an imago springs from the tattered pupa and wipes the floor with the opposition. What might be designated the Gee-I'm-A-Swan Syndrome.

When that I was and a little tiny boy, with hey-ho the wind and the colic, the twin hero-demons responsible for putting in this psychological spade-work were two paragons called Superman and Captain Marvel; the latter, of course, spent much of his time being Billy Batson, a teenage drop-out with an IQ of around nine, who, at moments of world tension, would cry "SHAZAM!" and turn into his barrel-chested alter ego, invulnerable to shot and shell and possessed of a moral constancy beside which St. Thérèse de Lisieux pales into insignificance. Superman's gimmick was to mope the streets as bespectacled Clark Kent until such time as he saw fit to step into the nearest phone booth, remove his natty gent's suiting, and emerge as a Rock of Ages, cleft for action.

PENNY PLAIN

Suckled at these heady teats, I spent many years in searching for the magic word that would, in my specific case, bring about the said transformation. After some routine inquiries, it turned out that the cry was "MONEY!" Particularly given the sort of society in which I was expected to live and move and have my being: a materialistic, empty, pelf-collecting, bourgeois etc. etc., where a bulge at the hip was worth two at the bicep. I had neither wish nor need to fly at the speed of light and lay out the full Great Train Robbery Team at a single uppercut; I merely wanted to be able to stroll through Burlington Arcade while merchant bankers and the better class of stripper fought to kiss the hem of my cheque book.

The one dream proved as unrealistic as the other; the requisite negotiable greenery was as hard to come by as bullet-proof skin. I learned to watch the wall, my darling, while the millionaires went by; I looked after the pennies, and the pounds looked after other people, and (since Man is more adaptable to his environment than the rest of the animals) I contrived to persuade myself that the popsongs were right, that I had the sun in the morning and the moon at night, that the best things in life were free, and that every millionaire would give his right yacht to change places with me. This belief was somewhat marred by the nagging suspicion that the characters who made their living writing such songs stored the public's recognition of their wisdom in three separate Swiss bank accounts, but I overcame it.

TUPPENCE COLOURED

It took me a short lifetime to realise that Rodgers, Hammerstein (both I and II), and G. Gershwin were all wrong, and that their catchy little anodynes weren't worth the wax they were gouged on. Because last week I walked into an unostentatious billet in Conduit Street, not unlike Clark Kent's mythic phonebox, and emerged, a mere magic moment later, as Superman; clad, I rush to add, not in velveteen jock-strap and aerodynamic cloak, but in a close-fitting sage-green 1968 Rolls-Royce.

Just to save trouble to those of you who are e'en this very minute knocking up begging letters in your head, I have to tell you that the aforementioned sage-green item was not handed over in return for the customary king's ransom; but lent, on a Cinderella contract requiring it to be brought back as hereinafter specified. Rolls employees are too discreet to let fall threats, but the glint in the well-bred eye left me quite clear that non-fulfilment on my part would bring the boys round with a sockful of sand, double quick.

Ernest Dichter and Lord Rootes, philosophers by appointment to the motor trade, have elsewhere noted the fact that cars mould the men that drive them; and this bizarre osmosis is as true, probably truer, where the best car in the world is concerned. Dangerously, the driver can come to believe himself the best man in the world. Which, given the materialistic lineaments of that world, in a curious way he is. And every feature of the car contributes to remind him of his eminence: a full technical inventory being available on request, let me illustrate this by reference to just one of the innumerable RR gee-gaws. Beside the steering-column is a small black button; press it, and the petrol filler cap opens by remote control. There is probably nothing which so accurately symbolises the relationship between the Rolls owner and the outside world than the remoteness of that control. It doesn't have a button to make the pump-attendant tug his forelock, but it comes pretty close.

I could hammer out a sizeable thesaurus on the sheer pleasure of shoving this automotive miracle around the landscape; I could remind you that the only way to tell whether the engine's actually running or not is to close your mouth over the exhaust; point out that you can hear nothing at a hundred mph except the sound of your beard growing; remark upon the singular fact that the seats adjust electrically (what else?) in the key of A-flat, I think it was. But why, when I've already gone to such unretractable lengths to establish the sort of flawful personality I am, should I bother to pretend that the joy of a Rolls is confined to its mechanical immaculacy?

I'd like to tell you about a traffic-jam: I spent forty minutes in one on the A40, an experience which, in other circumstances, would have left me perceptibly older and greyer and had the ulcers burgeoning over my duodenum like bubbles in a milk saucepan; but in the noiseless Rolls, I sat, dressed overall in a quizzical yet tolerant smile I've had stored up for years, but never dared use before, ears faintly cocked as, beyond the discreetly-tinted, electrically-shut windows, I picked up the excited yakking of lesser mortals in lesser cars asking one another the identity of this screen idol/oil sheikh/racehorse owner whom Destiny had allowed to glide, for a moment, into their tiny lives. When the jam finally broke, it was all I could do to stop myself driving down Whitehall, one hand slowly waving, to open Parliament.

But it's gone now, back to its legitimate owners, leaving me among the pumpkins; and I'm not sure whether to be glad for what I briefly had, or sorry for what I so quickly lost. If, as the admen say, cars are really mistresses, I had one night with Catherine the Great; which brings, if you'll pardon the expression, acute withdrawal symptoms. Who can follow her? Or, worse, guess at what the long-range effects of the experience may be? It is this uncertainty that makes the Rolls-Royce so dangerous.

Because all cars corrupt; but absolute cars corrupt absolutely.

*   *   *

A Lewes, Sussex, Corporation clerk has been sentenced to 18 months imprisonment for stealing 14,000 new penny pieces from Eastbourne public lavatories. He spent the pennies on high living.   *(Irish Times)*

Flatt & Mead, estate agents, of Tring, arranged a pentathlon in which four teams took part, including the National Westminster Bank, a local firm of solicitors and two directors of a local garage. The event began with nine holes of golf followed by darts and lunch.   *(Estates Gazette)*

"Stop racing your engine at her."

Yo Ho Ho and a Bottle of Sea Sickness Pills

LORD MANCROFT walks single-handed round his yacht

MY next yacht is going to be much bigger than my last. Actually there was some doubt in the upper echelons of the Bembridge Sailing Club as to whether a scruffy secondhand dinghy named "The Crab" ought to have been classed as a yacht at all.

In other respects, too, her debut had been inauspicious. The very day we acquired her she slipped her moorings, and, without any help from us, ran away to sea. The Coastguards apprehended her in the nick of time, and this was just as well because when Harry Hulbert's boat broke loose the previous week it ended up on the beach at Ostend, and Harry had to apply for an import licence to get her back. It was apparently thought that her return unlicensed might have prejudiced the British boat-building industry.

A contrite "Crab" was duly restored to us. We loaded her with thermos flasks, Norwich terriers, and other essential gear, and set course for Itchenor. Five minutes and two cable lengths later we rammed Lord Brabazon full amidships in *Tara*, and this was an encounter which not even the *Queen Mary* would have undertaken with impunity. Lord B. of T. was very nice about it. Well, fairly nice. It was generally understood, he reminded us, that the two most useless things in a small boat were an umbrella and a Naval Officer. But now (looking pointedly at me) he had a third candidate to put forward. And in any case, what was that I had on my head?

He was referring, I supposed, to my new green woollen pom-pom hat. I had bought it specially for the Bembridge Regatta, which is always a very pukka affair. Rear-Commodores and others stride around wearing white-topped caps and purposeful expressions. To appear amongst them bare-headed would, I felt, be inadequate, and to wear a white-topped cap would have been above my station. I suspected, however, that I must have misjudged the situation when the Bembridge police came into the Club and complained that the entrance was being blocked by a Rover car owned by a gentleman wearing a green woollen pom-pom hat. Clifton, our steward, replied sharply that no gentleman would ever wear a green woollen pom-pom hat. Apart from this the Bembridge folk were extremely kind, and I enjoyed my membership of their Club. Indeed, I find that my banker's order is still in existence even though I left the Island many years ago. I'm afraid, however, that I cannot agree with Ratty that there is nothing, absolutely nothing, better than simply messing about in boats. There is. Yachts, for instance—great big 100-footers, with six double bedrooms and colour TV. I could mess about in them for ever.

Of course there is a wide range of alternatives between *The Crab* and a 100-footer, and I have considered them all.

We don't want to get involved in anything like hard work; no blistered palms; no salt spray whipping through the hair, or any nonsense like that. The Prime Minister has not actually invited me to join the crew of his *Morning Cloud*, but if he were to do so I should have to decline. I am, however, comforted to read that you can disregard any of his orders as long as you say "Sir" at the end of your speech of resignation.

I have always thought that to own a racing yacht would be tantamount to tearing up five pound notes under a cold shower. Mr. Heath however is reported to have described *Morning Cloud* as a "bloody good investment". If so, it must be the first yacht to qualify as an investment since Noah built the *Ark*.

No round-the-world single-handed stuff, either. I am enchanted with my own company, but not when I'm being seasick.

A three-ton cabin cruiser? How many does that sleep in comfort? None. And what happens if you're cooped up with a lot of dear friends whom you find you loathe and you aren't due back until Wednesday week? This happened once to the late and sadly missed Lord Stanley of Alderley. He signed on an earnest young Welsh engineer as a deck-hand. Unhappily they fell out, and Ed Stanley berated him so soundly that the poor fellow threatened to put the matter into the hands of his solicitor as soon as they made Cornwall. "You may," said Ed calmly, "put the matter into the hands of your solicitor, or into any other portion of his anatomy which your ingenuity or his forbearance will permit." As soon, however, as they had tied up at Pendragon Creek the young man rushed to the phone box to tell his lawyer what had happened. With such Celtic volubility was he doing this that he failed to notice Ed creeping up behind him with a tool kit, and screwing him into the phone box. The boy was soon released because he had only to dial 999, or whatever it is you dial when an eccentric Peer of the Realm has immured you in a Cornish phone box. But the episode caused comment round Pendragon for quite some time to come.

So nothing cribbed, cabinned and confined for me. I shall acquire a yacht that'll make that little job of A. Onassis look like a Connemara coracle. I shan't worry about the cost because Mr. J. Pierpont Morgan tells me that if I have to worry about the cost of a yacht I obviously can't afford one. I shan't, of course, be paying British taxes because I shall be permanently tied up in Portofino or Antibes. This, after all, is the principal reason for owning a yacht. I have never heard of anybody owning a 100-footer that regularly put to sea. The Hohenzollerns and the Hapsburgs did not own yachts in order to go anywhere. They merely wanted to wipe the eye of the Czar, the Khedive, and King Edward VII.

I shall lack for nothing. Henri Sartori will be my private chef. The Amadeus String Quartet will play Mozart on the poop-deck. There will be lashings of caviare, and Charles Heidsieck Blanc de Blancs, and I must remember to find out what is the decimalised version of a lashing in case anything runs out. The Misses Taylor, Loren, Bardot, Lollobrigida, Ege and Welch will be my constant guests, and *The Financial Times* will arrive by air each morning. Bliss.

On second thoughts I shall have to put to sea once a year in order to avoid getting stuck for the local rates. I shall, of course, fly a flag of convenience so that I can't be held responsible if I get the charts upside down, and collide with somebody in the Channel. Whence shall I sail? Why, Bembridge, of course, though I shan't be able to get into the Harbour. Thanks to British Rail this is now silting up. I shall therefore have no problem with British yacht tonnage. This is calculated on the amount of square foot of deck open to the sun, and you have to pay about £1 a ton every time you enter a harbour.

It's a very complicated calculation. One of the chaps at the Admiralty whose job it was to do it eventually went mad and designed a yacht of such extraordinary proportions that its tonnage worked out at minus seven. He then sailed it all round Britain demanding £7 off the harbour-master at every port of call.

I shall hope to arrive off Bembridge in time for their annual Regatta, where the presence of my yacht may help to discountenance their uppity neighbours at Cowes. I shall, of course, say nothing about that banker's order. I shall just stand on the bridge, and touch my hat cordially to all my old friends as they sail past. And the hat, I need hardly add, will be green, woollen, and pom-pommed.

"My God, Arthur, we're not going to make it."

Losing Slimness the Easy Way

MAKE THE MACCLESFIELD MEAL YOUR CRASH DIET

Fattening diets have a way of being expensive and downright unpractical. What household is going to lay on a traditional English breakfast, a Continental lunch and a six-course dinner, *daily*.

You're put off the whole thing before you start. Or you do start, and next morning you're toying with a lettuce leaf.

So how about a crash diet you can go back to any time the surplus ounces seem slow to multiply?

It's a very simple diet indeed, even a homely one. It's called the Macclesfield Meal, though there's no record of it coming specially from that town, and it consists of a thick slice of cold suet pudding washed down with a pint of cocoa.

Have it eight times a day for three days, then weigh yourself. You may have gained only a few pounds, but that's a beginning. Now you can go on to an ordinary routine of bacon and eggs and roast beef, *and enjoy them as never before.* That's the beauty of the Macclesfield Meal, it actually sharpens the appetite for interesting food. But even when you've gone mad on ravioli and are sprinkling stuffed olives on your porridge, don't forget the occasional Macclesfield Meal to keep the scales going up and up.

HOW THEY DO IT
Some outsize personalities tell us their secrets

CLARE WHIBLEY, the huge romantic novelist, says serenely: "I think fat. So I am fat. Women have always had the ability to become what they wish to be.

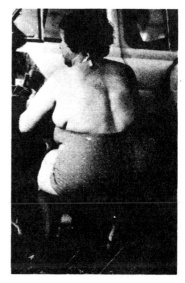

"I do have one tiny secret, though. I live on a twelfth-floor flat and always take the lift."

SIR MARVIN CHUNK, sometimes called the Big Daddy of Throgmorton Street, keeps his weight up by watching food commercials. "Since we got colour I've been following them seriously," he says, "with sensational results. I can't see a cross-cut chocbar, or a mound of field-fresh frozen peas topped with glistening country sausages, without dashing to the fridge for a bit of ice-cream or a cold potato. I read all the cookbooks too. Wasn't it Mar-

shall McLuhan who said 'Colour photography has done more for food than eating has'?'' **FRED FOSKETT,** beefy PR executive, found his weight going down smartly when he joined the firm. "I couldn't think why, with all the lunches, cocktail parties and dinners that go with the job. Then I realised that the job itself was to blame. I was working too hard. So I cut that down, and now I weigh the same as I did at university—fifteen stone.''

MUST I GIVE UP EXERCISE?
by Tom Plummer, famous TV sports fan

This is a question often asked by people trying to put on a bit of fat. Sometimes I've even heard them argue hopefully that muscles are weight, so if they build up their muscles they're getting heavier.

True, but it's not how to tackle the weight problem. You must stop thinking about muscles and take your exercise *in Nature's way*—that is, for the purpose of getting up a thumping appetite. And Nature will reward you generously, for a single currant bun will cancel a four-hour sprint round Regent's Park. Two buns, a plate of bread and butter and half a fruit cake—the sort of tea you'll be ready for after a sprint that long—will cancel it ten times over.

So take your exercise, by all means, as long as you put back what you take out. And, if you put it back at that rate, you soon won't be able to move, let alone sprint, and your problem will be solved.

ADVERTISEMENTS

YOUR LETTERS

I put on 8 lb. last Christmas. Yet I ate the same Christmas dinner as everyone else. It's just that I used my common sense, going easy on the turkey but making up with the stuffing and sausages.

I also had extra potatoes instead of sprouts, and did not waste valuable space on gravy but used it for bread sauce.

I was careful to put brandy butter, cream and sugar on the pudding, and chose nuts and fudge rather than grapes and Turkish delight. It's all a matter of will-power.

E. Beanwhistle, Mill Hill.

When I met my future husband I was 34-22-34. Yet within a week he "popped the question" and we have been happily married for nine years, with three lovely children, and my measurements haven't changed an inch!

My husband says he likes me slim, there's more room in bed and I don't wear out the carpets! And I say who wants to be fat, there's too much fuss made about it.

(Mrs.) L. Trinket, Dorking.

BOOK REVIEW

Fattening *(Harley Press, 15s.), by Dr. John Dunkin, will surely become the classic handbook on this subject. Expert in the field though its author is, he relies on getting his message over simply.*

"Remember," he tells us, "that in the 'sixties there were no thin people in Greasy Joe's diner off the Camberwell Road. And that the finest fattening exercise in the world is saying 'More, please'."

Writing about the thin patients who complain with tears in their eyes, "I can't put the weight on, doctor, though I eat like a pig," his comment is typical. "What bunk! Have they ever seen a pig eat? It stands in its food. I don't ask would-be fatties to do that, but they might at least squeegee the gravy up with a lump of bread."

"Look, Merrill, what a beautiful garden."

Some Corner of an English Field

ANNE SCOTT-JAMES

FEW would deny that there are more romantics per head of
the population in England than anywhere else on earth.
For every Englishman whose ambition is a powerful motor-car,
an executive suite, or a mink for his wife, there must be twenty
whose daydream it is to own a country cottage. Every weekend
the farms and villages of Britain swarm with hopeful couples
inquiring in pubs and poking about in barns and pigsties in
their search for a plot of land, an apple-tree and a tumble-
down house. The tumble-down-ness is an essential part of the
dream. The cottage-hunter's ideal is not a readymade house
with all mod. cons. He wants to use his creative faculties, to
get back to the workbench, to release his pent-up William
Morris instincts. His hope is to find something almost derelict
in a picturesque setting and to convert it, partly with his own
hands, which itch for a change from pen-pushing, into a personal nest.

His wife, mind you, may not be so keen. She may have
friends with weekend or holiday cottages who are in a state of
collapse from the strain of running two houses. The wife in a
weekend cottage situation spends Friday afternoon packing
food, Friday evening lighting fires and taking spiders out of
the bath, Saturday cooking and weeding, Sunday morning
cooking, Sunday afternoon locking windows and packing food
remnants and Sunday evening in the homebound traffic jam.
But there are still many innocent wives who share the
Englishman's dream of a country cottage. What chance have
these mad, romantic couples of finding one?

I am afraid that they have almost no chance of picking up
something for a song. In an overcrowded, inflationary island,
everybody wants land. A broken-down but repairable cottage is
a beautiful possession, and is usually sold by word of mouth,
friend speaking unto friend. For instance, the bachelor owner
of a gracious manor house with a penchant for giving elegant
Sunday luncheon parties might sell a cottage to a young friend
celebrated for his witty conversation. (Even so, he would be
more likely to let than sell, for today's witty conversationalist
is tomorrow's bore.)

Ah, says the cottage-hunter, but I am not thinking of a
fashionable neighbourhood. We would go somewhere quite
remote, like Herefordshire, Lancashire or Northumberland. In
fact, this makes no difference to the scarcity, and very little to
the price. London is not the only city in Britain. In Glasgow,
Birmingham, Newcastle and Bristol there are just as many
claustrophobic inhabitants longing for a country cottage who

scour the moors and farms as they are scoured in the south-east. If the cottage-hunter wants something for £5,000 or less, he must go somewhere *really* remote, like the north of Scotland or the wilds of Ireland or Wales.

In most districts, it is easier to find something already converted than something cheap and tumble-down. The price will probably be from £12,000-up for a "desirable residence" with main services and a bathroom. With any luck, the cottage will be fit to move into straight away, but the disadvantage will be that the converter's taste will not be yours. Removing the Devon fireplace with tiled surround, tearing out the wrought-iron light fixtures, and demolishing the pseudo-rustic porch will be irritating extras.

If you can't find a tumble-down cottage and can't afford a converted one, all is not lost. There are two other possibilities.

If a low buying price is important to you, you could consider an orthodox *modern* cottage, possibly semi-detached, which you could get in the region of £6,000. It won't be romantic. Your friends will not gasp with admiration at its old-world charm. But it will give you a bolt-hole. And with climbers up the house, shrubs and trees in the garden, and a Habitat décor inside, almost any house can be made palatable.

The other possibility is *not* to insist on vacant possession. This need not mean buying a cottage with an ancient inhabitant and waiting like a vulture for the poor old thing to die. You could take a pair of cottages, with vacant possession of one, or a terrace of four cottages, with vacant possession of two or three of them. The price will be much lower than it would be if the cottages were empty, and one day you yourselves, or, at worst, your children, will be the owners of a substantial piece of property.

Whatever sort of cottage you want, there's an art in looking. Give up those vague Sunday tootles in the car, trying one county after another. Select one area and work it like a pack of hounds. See the local agents not just once, but regularly. Study the local papers and get to know one or two local builders. Watch in "Country Life" for estates being sold and broken up. If you have upwards of £12,000 to spend, go to a London agent as well as to the local firms—agents like Hamptons have properties at this sort of price all over the country. And there is still, even today, the possibility of a stroke of luck. Hamptons know of a cottage in Somerset which was sold only a few weeks ago (admittedly in shocking condition) for £2,000.

If you have the money somewhere in the background but can't actually raise spot cash, you will probably get a mortgage. Most Local Authorities want to help, for they prefer inhabitated cottages to empty ones, which bring in no rates. (You won't get more than a two-thirds mortgage if the cottage is thatched.) Apart from the mortgage, you can usually get the standard grant for repair, up to a maximum of £500. On the subject of finance, don't be sloppy in your choice of builder.

Get at least three estimates for whatever work is necessary; the variation will astonish you.

I have already touched briefly on the drawbacks of a weekend or holiday cottage. Let me enlarge. The garden will always look a wilderness when you arrive, even if you left it exquisite last Sunday evening. You are sure to waste a lot of food; you will take home the cold joint, but not the half jug of milk and the odd tomato. You will spend many hours of your life travelling. The cottage will get damp in winter, and will be icy when you arrive. Socially, you will be neither fish, flesh nor fowl in the village. You may spend heavily at the fete and cut sandwiches for the cricket tea, but the part-timer is always a foreigner.

For some weekenders, the illusion fades. After a few years of cottage life, they pack up and go home and put the cottage on the market. (They will certainly have made a handsome profit.) But for many, what started as a holiday routine becomes a way of life, until they make their leisure cottage their permanent home. Men commute amazing distances in order to wake up to the sound of bird chatter, and women find that they can do without the alleged amenities of the city for the joy of living out of the rat-race. So the chances of finding a little old cottage with a plot of land and an appletree are not going to get easier as the years go by.

"See? Isn't this more fun than sitting around smoking pot?"

It's Quicker by Red Carpet

Says LORD MANCROFT

IT is better to travel hopefully, Robert Louis Stevenson assures us, than to arrive. I have never yet discovered what induced him to make this asinine pronouncement, though I realise, of course, that he lived before the age of the Jumbo-jet, the Inter-city express, and the T. & G.W.U.

Hope nowadays tends to languish when Trans-Siberian Airways regret to inform transit passengers of a further delay in the departure of their flight No. TSA 007 to Samarkand, and that this is due to operational reasons. (Operational reasons are to an airline what virus infections are to a doctor. You are to understand that neither of them has the faintest idea what has gone wrong.)

I doubt if R.L.S. ever had to sit for an hour outside Didcot station whilst British Rail, reluctant to admit that in the winter our weather tends to be wintry, struggled to unfreeze the points.

No amount of graft or low cunning, no friends in high places, nor the lushest of red carpets will get you out of this sort of mess. There are, in fact, two types of red carpet, the one upon which your ego can pose with pride, and the other which may genuinely speed you on your way. The merits of the two must be separately assessed.

The first type of red carpet was designed to be laid up to the carriage door of some prestigious traveller by coach or rail; but even the best laid carpets can go oft agley. The army manoeuvres which King Edward VII attended in Yorkshire during the Summer of 1909 had to be cancelled because of the English Summer weather, and the King returned to Harrogate station before the arrival of the Royal Train that was to take him across to Sandringham. In his kindly way he tried to put the Station-master at his ease, whilst that embarrassed official peered anxiously down the line, cursing the engine driver beneath his breath. "Tell me," said the King, "what will happen if, when the train does eventually arrive, the driver fails to pull my carriage up against the red carpet laid out here on the platform?" "Ee," replied the Station-master, tried beyond endurance, "Ee, let boogger try!"

Nowadays, the red carpet is seldom seen at railway stations unless you happen to be the sort of person who normally travels with four corgies. Privileges to a lesser degree, however occasionally, attend a Minister of the Crown. Once upon a time I was such a person, but it always worried me when, as I often did, I boarded a packed Cardiff train only to find that my secretary and I had been allotted an entire compartment to ourselves in order that we might discuss in secrecy the problems of unemployment amongst the slate-workers of Anglesey. No matter how much our unseated fellow travellers shook their fists, mouthed insults, or scribbled obscenities on the steamy windows, the guard refused to let them into our otherwise empty carriage. Some years later the improper thought crossed my mind that the guard, not sharing my political views, may have felt that all this parade of privilege could influence some votes.

That's one of the troubles about red carpets. The advantages they may bring to the beneficiary often seem to be at some other travellers' expense. "Good evening, Sir," says the airline P.R.O., smiling a P.R.O. smile, "a pleasant trip, I hope. Here, let me take your passport." Since you travel widely and your passport is consequently big with visas, you must appear glad to be relieved of this heavy burden. You are whipped through Immigration at the speed of light, pushing aside elderly nuns and chronic invalids. You are hustled conspiratorially down long draughty corridors, and you naturally reach the baggage collecting area well ahead of the crowd. But your beautiful rawhide suitcase takes just as long to come out of the bowels of the airport as does the elderly nuns' shabby grip, and all you'll have gained is a swollen ego at the price of some nasty looks.

It's the same on board a ship. You are nearly at New York's Pier 92. The baggage master, with a knowing glance, tells you that all is under control, and the Purser himself is looking after your papers. A private car has been laid on. Someone from the Consulate will attend. But as the ship is about to dock the familiar cry of "Everybody out" echoes along the quay, and a wildcat strike has you all, Duke and dustman alike, in its thrall. When it comes to carpets, the colour red means less than nothing to the unions.

The red carpet, however, means a lot to the ageing film star who needs the publicity, and to the retiring ambassador who has lived on protocol all his life, and wants to savour it for the last time. Air and shipping lines have a private code with which they mark their manifests, in the same way that a tramp will mark a door for the benefit of the next tramp to come along. If, say, Lord George-Brown, or Mr. Mick Jagger are travelling with us on Trans-Siberian, it will be known to all concerned how they are regarded by Cunard and BEA. Thus the precise way in which the carpet should be unrolled can be the more readily assessed.

A general assessment is fast becoming more difficult to make not because docks, airports and railway stations are growing more comfortable, or their staffs more efficient, but simply because the sheer bulk of modern travel makes it impossible to try and separate the sheep from the goats. When Euston Station first re-opened there were found to be no seats for passengers to sit on. This requirement had not in fact been overlooked. It was simply that the authorities didn't really want people to settle down and make themselves comfortable. They wanted passengers to come and go as quickly as possible, and thus make room for other comfort-lovers to take their place. They just wanted everyone to be equally uncomfortable.

In spite of this bizarre approach the travel authorities will never really run out of red carpet for the maimed, the sick and the blind, provided, of course, that they are given sufficient warning. What is actually wanted is a little less red carpet and a lot more good communication.

Couldn't T.S.A. have told me why my plane was delayed? I, too, am sorry that I was stupid enough to miss it when our flight was eventually called, but I'm not so observant as all those Pakistanis and au pair girls. The public address system is incomprehensible (even in English) and the closed circuit TV screen is practically invisible. And when I arrived, I know I hadn't warned anybody in advance that I'm badly lamed, but I wasn't lame when I disembarked from the aircraft at the end of a very slippery four-mile corridor.

I think all travellers should be regarded as VIPs, and all should be treated to the red carpet. The motto of the Green Star Line was alleged to have been "Passengers must not," and there are still some carriers who regard the passenger as an infernal nuisance rather than as their source of daily bread.

Ideally, then, all carpet should be equally red, and it may have been the unlikelihood of achieving this Orwellian bliss that was at the back of Robert Louis's mind. If, however, that day ever comes there will still be some people who for one reason or another are desperate to work their way to the head of the queue. For them new carpets must be devised, and old egos revalued. To those in urgent need of such preferential treatment, I commend a simple ploy. This calls only for the use of a small child, and the possession of an indelible red crayon.

Apply the latter to the face of the former in a series of irregular blobs. Then rub a moistened finger lightly over the face, in order to ensure uniformity. Grasp the child by the hand, advance boldly through the crowd, looking neither to left nor right, but pointing anxiously at the child whilst muttering the word *Masern,* or *rougeoles*, or *morbilio* or *sarampion* depending upon whether you are hustling through Germany, France, Italy or Spain. At any harbour, station, or airport where English is understood the word "measles" will suffice, and it will prove an equally effective red carpet.

❄   ❄   ❄

When the music for dancing is soft and the lights around are dimmed, there is more than just romance around, Birmingham police warned today.   *(Birmingham Mail)*

SUNDAY SAILORS:
THE GOOD SHIP SURBITON

by THELWELL

*"Only **you** could get becalmed in sewage."*

*"**I'm** not going to be rescued by Bob and Vera Harrington."*

"I still think Uffa's a damn silly name for a kid."

"You single-handed chaps are all the same."

171

SPRING

and

PORT WINE

In which **JOHN TAYLOR'S** fancy lightly turns to thoughts of booze

T HE pleasure of cooly observing the steady decline in a woman's resistance may be numbered among the most esoteric.

The gradual development from aloof formality into gale-force giggles; the encroachment of a warming glaze above the gimlet pupils; the cynical sudden revelation of an intimate confidence regarding a mutual female acquaintance—all these are welcome manifestations of the fact that you are at the beginning of a beautiful friendship.

It is not so much an indictment of our lack of originality as a clear proof of the method's efficaciousness that men still resort to liquor to effect the transition. And it is worth realising that because women will invariably trust the sweet-tasting drinks which agree with their sticky palates rather than the fiery warning jolt of basic spirits, that liqueurs are the readiest trap.

Half a pint of Advokaat slopped over her apple pie, clearly explainable as your own recipe for custard, has little subtlety but enormous effect. A succession of Grand Marniers alternated with a tumbler or two of Orange Curaçao may well have a brandy base; but compounded, as both are, of oranges, they must be absolutely crawling with Vitamin D. No girl who realises that beauty commences with good health will be able to resist your thoughtful considerations for her well being.

And as for Benedictine—isn't it made by monks? How could any girl come to harm by putting away half a bottle of a beverage brewed up by Men of God? *Pax vobiscum.*

But there is little sophistication in the liqueurs method, and to give that fifty-fifty chance atmosphere to the chase—which is the delicate appreciation of good hunting—there is no doubt that a shared bottle of wine offers the touch of togetherness which marks mutual respect between the tracker and his game.

The trick in wine drinking, therefore, is to ensure that you always drink slightly less than your guest; and the simplest way of ensuring such is by bringing to your own behaviour the ritualistic appreciations which have so long elaborated and spun out the simple swallow.

According to the French National Committee for Wine Publicity, for example, there is an approved pantomime for drinking a glass of wine, and my reader may be better informed by its reiteration:

"Tasting wine is a sacred rite to be carried out with gravity and serious attention," it says here. "First the sense of taste should be neutralised and the palate cleared with a little bread. Take neither water, cigarettes nor sweets.

"Fill the glass but half full, that the fragrance shall not disperse. Hold the wine up to the light to judge of its colour, clarity and brilliance, and then revolve the glass gently so that the wine swirls around and releases its fragrance. Insert the nose into the mouth of the glass and inhale the released *bouquet* fully . . . Then taste the wine in small breathtaking sips." How I wish I had been armed with such knowledge before I attended my own first wine tasting years ago.

I arrived with my invitation firmly clutched in my small hot hand and was confronted by a series of small tables stacked high with bottles, disciplined squads of empty upturned goblets, and small spartan dishes of dry biscuit.

"Then we had le coq au vin de Bourgogne, accompanied by a Chambolle Musigny, 1940."

Without instruction into the "sacred rites," it seemed to me that all one did was jug up from the first table and pass on as rapidly as possible to the next. I entered into the spirit of things readily and with an enthusiasm which mounted with each new bibulous experiment.

My enjoyment was to some degree lessened by the behaviour of those around me who seemed to be manifesting their critical faculties in a manner hardly less than ill-mannered. Wine of which, as it seemed to me, they disapproved, was given public opprobrium by the simple method of spitting it out into a handy bucket of sawdust. Determined not to look a gift horse in the mouth, and motivated partially by a sincere wish to assuage the wounded feelings of a host being treated churlishly, I felt it but good manners to swallow all that came my way with a polite smile of appreciation.

My confidence grew with my induction, and as the experts about me were acting out an esoteric little ritual of holding their glasses up to the light and swirling the wine deftly around inside it, I determined to follow suit.

Looking into the glare of chandeliers at a brimming wine glass held high above one's head is feasible provided a couple of pints of the vino hasn't already induced a latent vertigo. It needed only an unsteady pace backwards and an angular change of grip to have the glass slipping sideways and the wine coursing down my centre parting. The sharpened sense of humour of a man three parts gone enabled me to treat the catastrophe as a matter of noisy hilarity, but a wilful tenacity urged me to recharge my glass and try again.

This time, furthermore, I decided to elaborate my performance with a short demonstration of deft wine swirling.

The basic idea here is to rock the stem of the glass through an even axis—thus swooshing the liquid around the inside of its container supported by the sheer momentum of its speed. A notable similarity to the anti-gravity process may be found in the motorbike riders on a wall of death but—like the wall of death rider—uncontrolled speed can shoot the wine clear over the edge of the container and straight into tragedy . . .

I wrung out my shirt front as best I could, and partly conscious of an atmosphere of some antagonism among other guests decided to simplify my demonstrations into the surely manageable ritual of the aroma-sniffing.

I bent my head forward towards the wine glass and sniffed delicately—only to find to my sharp disappointment that it smelt of little other than wine, really. Persevering, I lowered my nose closer to the liquid and inhaled with the deep breath which results only from the practised years of a passionate life.

It was unfortunate that in my enthusiasm for my host's hospitality I had filled my glass rather fuller than the mandatory half-way mark. My nostrils submerged themselves well into the wine and the level in the glass went down like a water-butt sucked dry by a thirsty elephant.

No longer oblivious of the ill-will of those around me, I shook the wet hand of a thin-lipped host and repaired to the Cloaks, where I managed without undue effort to insert both my arms down the same sleeve of my overcoat.

As I turned to leave, the attendant who had extricated me from the strait-jacket of my own making touched his forelock with a fine humility, and pushed towards me with meaningful resolve a small saucer full of a collection of his own half-crowns.

I accepted one with thanks, pushed through the swing doors, and assuming all the circumspect dignity of the dreadfully drunk, made off in all directions.

*For many of us drinking is a
solitary pleasure.*

Yes, But Who's Minding the Yacht? WILLIAM DAVIS

Lipari

THERE'S a splendid yacht in the harbour here, owned by an English businessman. He ought to be happy, but he isn't. In fact, he is acutely miserable. He misses the office.

Back home he feels relaxed, confident, secure. Here he is ill-at-ease, lost, inadequate. He knows all about trade cycles, mergers, price-earnings ratios, and economies of scale—but very little about sailing. He knows how to squeeze a little extra profit out of German and Japanese customers, but has no idea how to handle the local traders. He suspects (as all wealthy people tend to do) that everyone is taking advantage of him. He doesn't particularly like the sea, he can't cook, and he can't speak Italian. Indeed, he can't do anything very much except sit on the deck and drink whisky. Which he does for most of the day.

Our friend's condition is far from unusual. Europe's beaches, just now, are full of paunchy businessmen sipping Scotch and asking themselves, "What the hell am I doing here?" It isn't easy to leave the rat race, even for a little while. It takes skill to do nothing, to be a bum. You can't be a frantic executive one day and a leisurely beachcomber the next: the contrast is too great. The bronzed, casual natives who make it look so simple have had years of practice. And they don't feel any guilt.

This guilt feeling is perhaps the biggest handicap. Doing nothing strikes many businessmen as immoral. If God had meant executives to be idle, he wouldn't have given them companies. How will the office cope without them? What will the shareholders say? How can the *country* prosper if its key people lie about in deckchairs?

Some try to get over this by taking files. They don't have to be about anything important; their comforting presence is enough. (It is, however, advisable not to take them along to the beach. I once saw a large, middle-aged German businessman chase a piece of paper which had, somehow, been blown out of his hands. Sweating profusely, he ran through the sand, stepping on brown, motionless bodies, destroying sandcastles, and leaving small children in tears. He caught it—but by the time he returned triumphantly to his chair, several other sheets had been blown away.)

Others keep telephoning the office. "Must keep in touch," they explain happily. In countries like Spain, Portugal and Italy, where the telephone is less than perfect, this can take up the entire day. You sit in your hotel room, staring at the telephone, waiting for the ring that will connect you with the familiar world you have so thoughtlessly abandoned.

If files have been forgotten, and the telephone is out of order, a standard ploy is to start running someone else's business. No hotel is ever run as efficiently as it should be; no restaurant ever reaches the right level of perfection. And, of course, the proprietor is just longing to have the benefit of your advice. Language may be a problem, but can generally be overcome by raising one's voice and speaking more slowly—the traditional British way of dealing with foreigners who are too lazy to learn English.

For really restless tycoons, the best answer clearly is to stay at home. You'd be surprised how many do just that. "Holidays?" they ask, amazed that you should even raise the possibility that they might indulge in anything so frivolous. "I haven't got time for that kind of nonsense. A couple of days at Christmas, that's all I ever need." They love feeling indispensable, and their business is usually structured in such a way that they really are. Everything depends on the man at the top, nothing is delegated, nothing is left to chance.

The snag, of course, is that sooner or later they tend to have an enforced holiday—in hospital. Suddenly it turns out that they are not indispensable after all; indeed, the company may actually do better.

Naturally we would not wish to see any Punch reader in such an embarrassing position. I have, therefore, conducted some extensive research on the subject of DOING NOTHING and herewith offer some answers to questions most people never dare to ask.

You say it takes skill to do nothing. How does one go about acquiring it?

Watch the experts; do some basic training. Women are often better at this than men, perhaps because they have more chance to practice. Get up an hour later than usual. Have yourself driven to the office. Buy an indoor golf set and give your secretary strict orders that you are not to be disturbed. (One well-known city tycoon used to play the violin for hours, but that seems too much like work.) Take a siesta. If anyone complains, tell them that you're "thinking". *Someone* has to do it.

But what about the country? What will happen to sterling if I relax?

Look at it this way. You've been working hard for years, right? You've done your best for Britain—*and we're still in a mess.* Perhaps it's time to give the other way a try.

"We should be weeding the herbaceous border."

Yes, well, I never did care that much for the Queen's Award anyway. But what about shareholders? How does one sell them on the virtues of doing nothing?

Tell them that you are going off to do some quiet long-term planning. Or that you are visiting an Italian subsidiary. (Some subsidiaries exist solely to provide directors with expense account sunshine.) The City will regard your absence as a sign of self-confidence: an indication that all is well and that your company is not a dreaded one-man band.

You may be right. But how can I make sure that there's still a desk for me when I get back?

Nail it to the floor. No, seriously, or at least half seriously, if you feel *that* insecure you ought to change your job anyway. Boardroom coups are not that common; in any case, one hopes you have at least one colleague who can be relied upon to protect your interests.

People need a holiday from each other. Give your colleagues a chance to miss you: they will appreciate you all the more when you get back. Weary, harassed executives tend to make bad judgements, alienate colleagues, offend customers, wreck relationships. Doing the wrong thing is worse than doing nothing.

Agreed. Let's deal with guilt. I take it you don't regard leisure as immoral?

Certainly not. Work is a means to an end, not an end in itself. It's immoral *not* to take time off. Ask your family. If you must feel guilty, let it be about the way you neglect them. Sit on that beach, waste that week. Tell yourself that it's all for their benefit: you'll feel infinitely better.

That's easy for you to say. You haven't seen my bills.

No, and I don't want to, thank you. But you'd be amazed how many people manage to cope without doing a thing. Invest your money, let others work for you. The Stock Exchange will tell you that you're doing Britain a service: you are "keeping the wheels of industry turning". You don't have to believe it; the point is, it works.

All right. Let's get back to your friend in the harbour. What would you advise him to do?

First, sell the yacht. It's far better to know someone who has a yacht, and cadge an invitation, than to maintain your own. Secondly, stay in one place. Moving around requires an awful lot of quite unnecessary effort. Thirdly, let someone else deal with the local traders: lie in the sun and forget about being a Big Man. Fourthly, rediscover books, and of course, Punch.

Trust you to work in a plug. But let's see if you take your own advice: describe a typical day.

Fair enough. Last Wednesday's diary: 10 a.m. Woke up. Thought about coffee. Went back to sleep.

11 a.m. Should I shave? Why?

11.30 a.m. Had coffee. Looked at sea.

Noon. Thought about lunch. Felt sorry for colleagues back in the office.

"Half-an-hour's rest after meals."

1 p.m. Called taxi to take me to restaurant.

3 p.m. Had a siesta. Very civilised institution; can't think why we in Britain neglect it.

4.30 p.m. Swim, followed by an hour comatose in the afternoon sun.

6.30 p.m. Read two chapters of *Rabbit Redux*. Thought about dinner.

8 p.m. Called taxi to take me to restaurant.

10 p.m. Sat on terrace, drinking brandy and listening to Sicilian songs.

11 p.m. Bed.

A full day, you will agree. Calling the taxi, I admit, required a bit of an effort and the swim was rather too strenuous.

But nobody is perfect.

You didn't get bored?

No. Next question.

Do you think doing nothing could become a habit?

Yes. Next question.

You're not ashamed of being so lazy?

You must be joking. Next question.

Will you try to keep it up when you get back home?

I'll be honest with you. I wish I could. It's very pleasant to be a bum: seen from here, it seems a compliment rather than an insult. The young, today, are much better at it than their parents ever were. They are not afraid of a little self-indulgence: prosperity has brought freedom.

Alas, I'm weak. If God had meant me to be idle, he wouldn't have made me editor of a magazine. Holidays are fine, but I don't really want to spend the rest of my life doing nothing. How would the office cope without me? What would the shareholders say? How can the country prosper if I spend all my time in a deckchair?

Ablutions Down
The Arches of The Years
In which PATRICK RYAN tells the tale of total immersion

WHEN richer readers and more pampered writers get to Tokyo for Expo 70, they may find it immortally rewarding if they ask their hall porter for directions, not to the nearest geisha house, but to the hotel just outside the Nipponese capital which has installed a solid gold bath. The proprietor charges 1,000 yen or about twenty-five bob for a two-minute dip in this precious tub, and this swift ablution is considered by local legend to add three years to the customer's life. Fuller instructions as to how to find this promise of eternity are hampered on this Anglo-Saxon page by the sukiyaki quirk that the land of the rampant egg-yolk favours neither names for its streets nor numbers on its houses.

The process of immersing the human frame in some medium other than air for purposes of cleanliness, though currently highly popular, has had its fashionable ups and downs. Perhaps our latter-day Western obsession for daily washing dirt from off the epidermis is motivated by a Pilatian need to lave ourselves symbolically of other people's blood, or of the taint of polluting our planet. The earliest bath thus far discovered was in the Palace of Minos in Crete and indicates that the gentry liked a hot soak even 3,600 years ago. The Greeks were partial to thus sluicing off the sweat of Olympian strife, and the Romans might still now be occupying Hadrian's Wall and 10 Downing Street had they not allowed their imperial barbarism to be dulcified by a surfeit of nightingale's tongues and lolling about in hot water.

But our Early Christian Fathers took a more ascetic, if less nasally attractive point of view. St. Benedict, in the sixth century, came firmly down on the side of the great unwashed with his command to his followers that "to those that are well, and especially to the young, bathing shall seldom be permitted". It may well be as a result of this edict that the Benedictine Order became known as the Black Monks. St. Agnes, the patron saint of young virgins, went to heavenly glory in an odour of sanctity reinforced by the effluvium of never having washed her body in her life. As she passed through the golden gates, St. Peter remarked how fortunate for all angelic nostrils that she was only thirteen years old when blessed with holy martyrdom. But nevertheless, St. Francis of Assissi listed dirtiness as one of the outward marks of holiness, and St. Jerome publicly rebuked his adherents for keeping themselves too clean.

Perhaps heeding this saintly advice, but more likely deterred by the outside temperature and lack of central heating, the early British didn't go a bundle on total immersion. Henry IV did his bit to keep the court salubrious by making a ceremonial bath, as well as the all-night vigil, an obligatory part of the ritual of installation into knighthood. When this purifying ablution ceased to be generally observed and simple dubbing was deemed sufficient to make an aristocrat, knights who had gone through the watery initiation were known as "knights of the bath" to indicate their precedence over their unwashed peers who had been made up mucky. The present Order of the Bath was invented by George I in 1725 and capitalised in its title on the ancient term of distinction. Its members have nothing to do with scrubbing royal backs with diamond-studded loofahs or any other intimate duties in the Queen's bathroom. Which is perhaps just as well since the order can have 1,878 members and she'd need a *salle de bain* as big and draughty as the Albert Hall to accommodate them.

Her eponymous predecessor, Elizabeth I, was considered surpassing sanitary in her time because she took a bath once a month "whether she needed it or no". Despite the innovation of the Order of the Bath, a Georgian duke later pronounced that it was sweat, dammit, that kept a man clean. And it may have been adherence to this hygienic principle which resulted in there being no bath fitted in Buckingham Palace when Queen Victoria came to the throne in 1837. Aided, perhaps, by the teenage influence of Florence Nightingale, who expressed the conviction that "with privacy and a quart of water, any woman can be clean".

The bath made a triumphant come-back in Britain, however, during Victoria's reign, due perhaps in equal parts to the cumulative effect of John Wesley's heretical teaching that "cleanliness is next to godliness," major improvements in the efficiency of plumbing, and the fact that the Industrial Revolution made life in general much grubbier.

In addition to simple hot water, people have since submitted themselves to baths in mud, peat, bran, malt, soup, offal, blood, dung and most other non-corrosive emulsions. Historical awards for originality have gone to Poppaea, Nero's wife, who tubbed herself in asses milk, Mary, Queen of Scots, who soaked her long body in white wine, Cora Pearl who disported before customers in champagne, and Mrs. Porter and her daughter who washed their feet in soda water. The late Aga Khan's bath-water was probably the most valuable since hotel fable holds that special catchment arrangements had to be made when he was in residence so that it could be bottled and sold to the faithful as a universal panacea. Besides their normal ablutionary function, baths have been used by Romans for committing hara-kiri comfortably in, by apocryphal Cockney flat-dwellers for keeping the coals in, and by Mr. George Joseph Smith for doing-in brides in.

The most booming type of bath at the moment is the sauna, and devotees may be interested to know that it derives from the Scythian baths described by Livy, who relates that these inhabitants of Southern Russia in the last century BC used to throw hempseed and water on to hot stones to produce intoxicating fumes in the bath-house. Marijuana is made from the hemp plant, *cannabis sativa,* and it looks as if the wily Scythians gathered at the sauna not only for a neighbourly sweat but also for a communal joint of pot . . . Mr. Lennon, art tha listening in the lavatory there below?

But the very latest self-laundering status symbol is the "Sagittarius Double Bath" which has a dunking area of twenty-four square feet and is a luxury bubbletub built for two. It costs about £270 basic and several hundred have already been sold by its British designer to happily-splashing customers. The bridal suite at a Cape Town hotel has a double-bath as its main attraction and other international hostelries have them on order.

Not only does the double-bath facilitate getting your back scrubbed, and permit the singing of steamy tenor-soprano duets, but it also makes searching for the soap a great deal more interesting. The only possible fly in the foam is the old superstition that if two people wash themselves in the same water, they will quarrel before next nightfall and some misfortune will befall one of them. And the traditional method of averting such malignant retribution is for one of the pair to spit in the dual-purpose water. Ladies, of course, do not expectorate in company, and Hugh Hefner considers that there are few male actions better calculated to whip the kimono back onto an amiably-naked doxy than to have her would-be tub-mate spit in her bath-water.

*   *   *

The Kangaroos Are Fine, I Like the Cricket, But Could You Show Me Something a Little Smaller?

ALAN COREN goes to buy an island

I rang Harrods. You can buy an elephant at Harrods, and there must be more islands in the world than elephants.

"Harrods Estate Office," said Harrods Estate Office.

"I'm looking for an island," I said.

"Town ór country," said the switchboard. Either she had not heard me aright, or else that is the automatic response down in Hans Road when madmen spring from their earpiece. Not that the idea of a town island was so unpleasant, at that; I am an urban soul at root, and a poor sailor, and if they had something close to South Audley Street with a palm or two on it and a clement air, it might have suited me very well. I could even keep my present phone number, and since the future might well be filled with holding off crocodiles and keeping my head from the shrinker's crucible, any reduction in inconveniences would be very welcome. But I doubted my chances.

"Country, I suppose," I said.

There were some clicks, and a handsewn voice slid on.

"I should like to buy an island," I said.

"What sort of island did you have in mind, sir?" he said.

This was promising. I might have been in the shirt department. No doubt a runner would come round with a swatch of samples—a few assorted beakers of sand, views from a dozen different volcanoes, an edible crab or two, a selection from their wide range of atolls.

"The Mediterranean, perhaps?" I opened. In fact, I rather fancied something of a Balinese order, but I hardly knew the man and did not wish to appear flash. We might work eastwards later.

But "Ah," he said, "Oh," he continued, the chagrin tangible as drizzle. "I'm afraid we only have UK properties here."

I thought of waves dashing on Welsh offshore rocks, and my heart dancing with the Scilly daffodils. Of harsh, healthy mornings in the Hebrides, with their lucrative fauna. *Tarka The Puffin, Alan Coren's warm human story of a lonely man and a short bird, now in its eighteenth impression, £3.50, illustrations by the author, you saw the film now read the book.*

"That might do, in fact," I said, snapping out of it. "I need a retreat, a quiet spot, a place to think. Do you have anything in that line?"

He went away. Far drawers opened and shut. He came back.

"Very little, I'm afraid," he said. "A couple off the South-west coast of Ireland, very small. There's such a demand."

There was bound to be. Whenever I decided to buy anything, it always turns out to be at the height of a boom, in the eye of a trend. The last time it was long-case clocks. Before that, Suffolk rectories.

"Nothing else?" I said.

He lowered his voice.

"You might try Knight, Frank and Rutley," he said, "it's more their line."

"Pity," said either Knight, Frank or Rutley. "A few months earlier, we could have shown you Bardsey Island. Off the Welsh coast. It was actually a kingdom, as a matter of fact. Had a throne on it."

There you are. Some men spend their lives grovelling for peerages, sucking up to the donors of undistinguished gongs. And, but for the caprice of time, I could have been an entire king. *Good evening, this is King Coren I speaking, I'd like a table near the door for 8.30.*

"What did it fetch?" I asked. Said, it seemed a crass question. Realms falling beneath the gavel. Sceptre and crown must tumble down, and in the dust be equal made.

"Ninety thousand," he said.

It seemed a small price to pay for the cornerstone of an empire. I am young, after all, and have read history in my time: what was the British Empire, once, but hundreds of Bardseys and Mercias and Wessexes and the like. You'd probably get a good mortgage on a kingdom (there must be blokes at the Abbey National who'd do anything for a dukedom), you could settle in, raise a small army, engage in forays against local rock-clusters, work your way up. It was a far cry from my original vision of lolling among windfallen coconuts and waiting for nude lady cartoonists to wade ashore, but more appealing by far.

"You have nothing else like that at the moment?" I enquired.

"I'm afraid not," he said. "There's a big demand."

"I know," I said.

"We have one or two at around twenty thousand," he said, "off Ireland. Nothing on them, of course, and a bad approach. Only accessible to helicopters, really."

That seemed less than idyllic, on the one hand, and an unlikely power-base, on the other. A bare rock, with just me and a Sikorsky on it, waiting for the cloud to lift. I put this to Sir Frank Rutley, as I had come to think of him.

"There's always John D. Wood," said Sir Frank.

They're a chummy brotherhood, estate agents.

"It so happens," said John, "that we may be in a position to offer you an offshore Irish island for £120,000."

"Really?" I said, in a cool-headed voice designed as a rampart thrown up around my overdraft.

"Five hundred acres," said John.

I've never been too hot on acreage. I've always had to visualise my old school playing-field (two acres) and multiply by the number required to reach the total. The one-twenty-grand job seemed big. You could hold, for example, four hundred simultaneous football matches on it, if my memory served me right.

"Perhaps you could send me details?" I said nonchalantly.

"Of course, sir," said John. "You *are* Irish, I take it?"

"No," I said. "Why?"

"Oh. Well, the Irish government rarely grants permission to foreigners to hold more than five acres in Ireland."

"This isn't in Ireland," I said. "It's off it."

"De facto," he said, flawlessly, "but not de jure."

I had known, before the whole thing started, that at some point I should have to wrestle with legalities. That point had come. I thanked him, and rang off.

There was much I needed to know before proceeding further. I like dreams as much as the next man, but they have to have at least the possibility of realisation. And just how insular *was* an island? Did they all belong to someone, some government, some monarch? Could I make my own laws, and, if so, how far could I make them? Could I arrange my own tax system? Could I introduce the guillotine? Droit de seigneur, coinage, slavery? If I bought an Ionian beach, could I practise polygamy there? If something in Hudson's Bay was to be my territorial lot, could I make fir-cones the currency and rock the international monetary scene by devaluing the dollar?

I left the telephone and went to Wildy's, a bookshop nestling by Lincoln's Inn, that has spent the last century or so piling incomprehensible jargon onto shelves so that the legal profession may keep the layman at bay and the wolf from the door. One look at the towers of international law was enough to tell me that not only should I never be able to define a sovereign island and find out what I could get away with on it, but also that the juridical world was just waiting for a mug like me to drop anchor off my acquisition: one footprint on the beach, and the International Court at The Hague would have enough to keep them in work for a generation.

For they were the lads to worry about. For those of you about to embark on the course outlined heretofore, may I recommend Edvard Hambro's *La Jurisprudence de la Cour Internationale*? It runs to around seven vols so far, is written in legal French, costs about forty quid, and is probably a mine of information. If they ever get me on *Desert Island Discs* and ask me for the one book I'd take to keep my inexhaustible needles company, that'd be it. For it is to the International Court that blokes are haled whenever they overstep the territorial mark, and it is there that such things as countries are defined.

I asked for something a mite more portable, and was led to

185

The Acquisition Of Territory (R. Y. Jennings, Manchester University Press, £1.20). The book was a revelation, packed with invaluable minutiae about the possibilities of my acquiring an island by force (something that Harrods, Sir Frank, and John D. had cunningly neglected to tell me through jealousy, no doubt, of their commission) and hanging on to it. Some ninety per cent of Professor Jennings's succinctitudes lay outside my vocabulary, but here and there, as I flipped, telling phrases leapt from the page to rivet the eye and buoy up the spirit. Shall I ever forget *titulus est justa causa possidendi quod nostrum est,* which even O-level translators may fairly render as *what we have we hold?* In brief, having landed on my island, whether backed by mortgage or bayonet, it was up to any spoilsport objecting to the way I ran my seraglio or thumbscrewed my Nubians or exploded my nuclear devices to get me off by force or writ. Even if I came under the nominal ownership of Britain, say, or France, or any one other so-called sovereign state, there was nothing to stop me declaring UDI, and leading a full and happy life, provided I kept one ear open for the approaching gunboats and scanned the skies for parachuting QCs. And the likelihood of a major power so stirring it was pretty remote, since there was no way for them to know whether I shouldn't then run with my hard-luck story to another major power who would then take over the defence, represent my case at the UN, and do any number of inimical things.

The money to be made, against your initial stake of, say, £120,000 is limitless. Declaring your own laws, like no extradition, no booze duty, no drug restrictions, and so forth, would enable you to entertain the world's dregs at unboundaried profits, out of which you could pay top rates for the hired guns necessary to keep the tenants in line and kill insurrection in the nest.

I went back to the phone, trembling like Hitler on the Calais cliffs. The world my oyster, packed from lip to lip with pearls. I rang the Greek Embassy (would *they* dare challenge me if I set up a democracy some twenty miles offshore, would the International Court evict me in the face of their great

"An excellent meal. My compliments to the gardener."

liberal tradition, would the Afro-Asian bloc not rise as one at
the UN if the junta tried to close my lefty haven?), and I was
transferred from desk to desk down the long consular
corridors, and eventually someone came up with a name who
knew a name who handled the sale of things in the wine-dark
sea.

"Is Stakros speaking," he said.

"I am looking for an Aegean island," I said. "Or possibly
Ionian."

"Is both very nice," said Stakros. "You wish with planning
permission for hotel development, with villa on, with sandy
beach, with resident domestics, very clean girls, also traditional
cooking, what sort island you want?"

I want a base for empire, Mr. Stakros, I thought, I want a
spot convenient for second fronts, a launching-pad to Turkey
and the rich spices of the Orient, a fortress with a quiescent
population who have been waiting for a leader all these years,
muscley, hard-eyed men who know not fear and can handle
the Tereschnikov 7.65 mm machine-gun that the Russians will
be glad to give me when they hear what I have to say, and the
Sidewinder missile that the Americans will give me when they
hear what the Russians have to say, an island with a rocky
conference hall and a heli-pad for wheedling heads of state to
come and woo me on. Let Hugh Hefner and Compton
Mackenzie and David Hemmings and Huntington Hartford
buy their hideaways and tax-havens, Mister Stakros, I have
bigger fish to fry.

"Oh, just send me anything you have," I said.

That was yesterday. The postman hasn't called yet, but I
heard a letter-box clunk a door or two away, and he will not
be long.

Attila started small.

The New Chair of Leisure

Prof. DAVID WILLIAMS
delivers his inaugural address

VICE-CHANCELLOR and comrades, I'm sure you'll excuse me if I address you from a recumbent position in my genuine hide-covered, down-stuffed swivel-chair with lapis-lazuli trim and matching stool. Be imaginative, Comrades, and think of me as a Symbol: the recumbent incumbent in fact. After all, if you've been elected to a professorial Chair why not lie in it? Anyway, I don't propose to keep you long: I'm due to be thrashed by my wristy and delicious Sauna lady in half an hour.

And don't let anybody take notes. Taking notes means evidence and I hate evidence. It can also get you into an anxiety-state about not keeping up. And this Lecture-hall is no place for anxiety-states. As Pheidias said to Aristides, his eager, nail-biting architecture-student: "Don't copy me, buster. Go and build your own Acropolis somewhere else. And why stick to Acropolises? I see they're advertising for somebody to fix them up with a wailing wall in Jerusalem. Why wailing I hear you say. Search me, boy. But why not book yourself on the next trireme and case the joint? It could be a challenge." Or as Toulouse-Lautrec (I have to get some culture into this, Comrades) said to an over-zealous disciple: "Imitation will get you nowhere, boy. Find yourself another brothel and draw your own debauches. Blow your own strumpet in fact."

At any moment between now and 4 p.m., Comrades, feel free to nod off, or do your own mind-boggling. Anyone signing on for this course does so by writing a cheque, not a thesis.

Keeping always firmly in mind the undoubted fact that going downhill is an uphill job, I shall try, during the opening term of the course, not to make my list of prescribed books too burdensome. No one can be expected to empty his mind of everything, including cant, and at the same time keep soaking up the printed stuff. So I thought on the drama side we might take a bleary look at *The Playboy of the Western World* by J. M. Synge. This harks back to the Irish way of life shorn of the gelignite, makes the most of the allure of a layabout called Christy Mahon, and has a woman in it called Pegeen Mike who isn't a bit like Bernadette Devlin and who'd never have dreamt of pummelling Sir Henry Campbell-Bannerman with her tiny fists. We shall also pay particular attention to the works of that unique poet Edmund Clerihew Bentley who wrote of Edward the Confessor that he "Slept under the dresser./When that began to pall/He slept in the hall". Then there is that splendid novel by Jules Verne called *Twenty-thousand Leagues under the Sea* which is restful because none of the characters can be got at by telephone. Shakespeare I think we should get in somewhere so I suggest *King Lear,* with its shuddery representation of what a dog's life a man can lead when he hasn't the sense to leave well alone.

The subject you are about to study under my deliberately unobtrusive direction has its difficulties. No one can derive the full benefit from doing nothing without at the same time giving the appearance of doing something. Total inactivity—lying on your back in the park with a Sunday newspaper tented over your face to keep off a momentarily appearing sun for example—is inelegant and arouses opprobrious comment. "Big strong bloke like him, he should be oiling the minute-hand of Big Ben or hosing down protest-marchers"—you know the sort of thing. So have perhaps some unfinished tapestry-work on hand, if you are gaily liberated; this you can snatch up on becoming observed. Or if you are ordinarily masculine have an old boot and hammer beside you and keep your mouth full of nails. These by the way have a pleasant tang to them, a bit like asparagus, but think before you swallow.

Remember that in the long run nothing is more restful than watching other people work. Do not therefore toast in the sun or loll in the sea at Corfu, Cannes, the Cape of Good Hope or similar, because everybody else will be at it too. The moment you lift your towel off its oblong, a prowler .with no fixed abode, skilled after fifty consecutive weeks' experience of finding a tenantless parking-meter in the EC4 precinct, will have homed on to it. No, the really riveting thing is riveting, so take your hols along the Upper Clyde where you can watch tankers grow visibly, spot lame ducks keeping up their paddling in oily waters, and even glimpse Jimmy Reid who will be aye talking.

While I'm on my bottom I might also mention career-prospects in this field of study. "Career" is an unappetising word and I use it only as a sort of regretful shorthand. But there may come a time when the less adroit student can drum up no further public financial support for more research into the lifestyle of the drone or into the B (bloodier) text of Beowulf, and will have to leave the warm nest.

To these disadvantaged ones I say: keep on trying. Your prospects may yet be good. Bear continuously in mind, for

189

instance, a clerkship in the Ministry for Imperial Affairs. Or how about rate-collecting in a No Go area? Keep lobbying the Ministry of Culture about their ludicrously inadequate research grants. Tell them you look like being' hung up for at least 18 months at page 10 of your "Finnegans Wake Makes a Good Read if you Take it My Way". Don't sniff at umpiring. Cricket? Quite a possibility. Only you must of course insist on an electric go-cart when officiating at any match where a right- and a left-arm bowler are used in combination. Chess? What could be more restful? Offer to accompany Spassky on a world-tour, but have a heavy cold of course if he ever again gets landed with Bobby Fischer.

No. I want no gloom at this Inaugural. Think it out well ahead and I can see restful futures ahead for most of you provided there's no return to square-bashing and sergeant-majors as in the decadent days gone by. Excuse me now. I see my luscious Sauna-girl Hypatia peeping in. She beckons, and I wouldn't miss my birching, no, not for all the PhDs in the Guide Michelin.

"You can't help but like them—they don't care a damn."

Calling all A. A. members—
this is your interpreter speaking

JONATHAN ROUTH

AA Members Handbook 1972/73.
Automobile Association. 60p.

I quote from this work, the Yellow Book of our day:

★★★★★ **Claridges** Brook St W1 ☎01-629 8860
205rm(205⊂₤) Lift ♪ 📺 TV ⌐₂ Ldmidnight
B⊂₤15.10 L₤2.85alc D₤3alc S15%

So, let us now be very patient and interpret.

It's a five-star place (more appropriate really if five crowns had been used), it has a name, an address, and a telephone number.

★★★★★ **Claridges** Brook St W1 ☎01-629 8860
205rm(205⊂₤) Lift ♪ 📺 TV ⌐₂ Ldmidnight
B⊂₤15.10 L₤2.85alc D₤3alc S15%

It has 205 bedrooms, and 205 men permanently soaking in baths. Unless this is a pictorial euphemism for 205 lavatory attendants. Or maybe it means there's a framed reproduction of that picture of the Murder of Marat in his Bath on the wall of each of the 205 bedrooms. Or that when all the 205 bedrooms are full the staff will be happy to make up beds in baths for a further 205 guests. The meaning of this symbol is not crystal clear. It's the first time that the AA have branched out into this form of artwork, and I suspect they gave their artist too free a hand. Why is the man in the bath? Surely the sort of person who goes to Claridges is not accustomed to storing coal in his bath and therefore needs this clue as to the correct use of the receptacle? I find it baffling. The man himself looks surprised, as though he's been caught doing in the bath something people don't normally do in the bath. The AA Disciplinary Committee would do well to consider his continued appearance in their handbook.

We continue:

★★★★★ **Claridges** Brook St W1 ☎01-629 8860
205rm(205⊂₤) Lift ♪ 📺 TV ⌐₂ Ldmidnight
B⊂₤15.10 L₤2.85alc D₤3alc S15%

Claridges has a lift. Good. But it's a lift followed by a moon symbol—a romantic lift, for lovers; it operates only at night; Juliet's balcony gliding up and down the Brook Street facade of the hotel.

Or, the liftman's a loony. "The lift has stopped, sir, not as you suggest through my turning off the current, but because of a genuine mechanical failure. And it's laid down in regulations, sir, that the procedure to be adopted in such a circumstance is for the lift operator and all passengers to strip off all their clothes and do heavy breathing until rescued. See, sir, with my previous experience I can completely undress in 23 seconds flat . . ."

But it isn't that. The moon symbol means there's a Night Porter on duty. With any luck he's a loony, too. You'll know

191

for sure if he turns out to be the man lying in your bath.

★★★★★ **Claridges** Brook St W1 ☎ 01-629 8860
205rm(205🛁) Lift ⓧ ⑳ TV ⨂ Ldmidnight
B🍳£15.10 L£2.85alc D£3alc S15%

On.

This is more difficult. A section of accordion I would guess.
It means the loony night porter can be summoned to come to
your room and play the instrument—if he's not occupied in
serenading couples travelling in the lift by moonlight, that is
. . . Or does it simply mean central heating, a radiator? If you
still want an accordion that's the first place I'd look behind.

★★★★★ **Claridges** Brook St W1 ☎ 01-629 8860
205rm(205🛁) Lift 🆇 ⑳ Ⓣ🆅 ⨂ Ldmidnight
B🍳£15.10 L£2.85alc D£3alc S15%

TV—that's simple enough. An old-fashioned entertainment
for those who don't want to get involved with the loony
accordionist. But wait. It's followed by an impaled dog's head.
Definitely a dog of the hound variety. They are eccentric, some
of the old county families who put up at Claridges. "I've told
you, Sir Jocelyn, you may stable your horse in the mews
behind, but we cannot allow the public corridors of the second
floor or the television lounge to be used as an exercise pen for
a whole pack of hounds . . ."

I suspect the AA is trying to suggest that Claridges reserves
the right to adopt stern measures against patrons who try to
smuggle in packs of hounds.

★★★★★ **Claridges** Brook St W1 ☎ 01-629 8860
205rm(205🛁) Lift 🆇 ⑳ TV ⨂ Ⓛdmidnight
B🍳£15.10 L£2.85alc D£3alc S15%

So we come to Ldmidnight—Ladies are expected to be out of
Gentlemen's Rooms by Midnight, surely? It's good to discover
there are still places in the permissive society where the old
standards are adhered to. They can't be serious, can they? No.
"Ldmidnight" (pronounced "DIEKNEE") is a delicious
Norwegian cheese, the speciality of Room Service ever since
the late King Olaf demanded 14 kilos of it for breakfast. It's
the traditional food of travelling Norwegian accordionists, and
you will find tidbits of Ldmidnight brought on when the
loony night porter comes to play in your room.

Sadly, if we refer to Abbreviations and Symbols we find that
the prefix "Ld" means the time last dinner can be ordered. But
you can still ask if they've got some Norwegian cheese.

And just before the prices, which make as much sense as any
prices do these days, we get this big B followed by that man in
the bath again. Obviously—breakfast served in your bath.

I said the fellow looked as though he was doing something
one doesn't normally do in the bath. Digesting his kipper off a
plate on his knee. The place is bulging with eccentrics.

Claridges, from this account, just isn't how I imagined it at
all. These roaming packs of hounds, crazy accordionists, loony
liftmen. It's surprising how much extraordinary information
they can pack into these brief entries in the Handbook.